Love is Boundless

Love is Boundless

Sabrina Pérez

thesabrinaperez Enterprises Ltd. Co.

ISBN: 979-8-218-26676-9
Published August 8, 2023

**thesabrinaperez Enterprises Ltd.
Co., 2023**

Disclaimer:

The information and advice contained in this book are based upon the research and the personal and professional experiences of the author. They are not intended as a substitute for consulting with a healthcare professional. The publisher and author are not responsible for any adverse effects or consequences resulting from the use of any of the suggestions, preparations, or procedures discussed in this book. All matters pertaining to your physical health should be supervised by a healthcare professional.

Love Notes & Praise

"Your words of wisdom have helped me self reflect in my healing process. Your support has been a crutch to lean on when I have felt alone."
- Gabriella

"I have some young girls that NEED to read this. You have a special gift. Thank you for sharing it. Vulnerability looks great on you. Looking forward to more of your thoughtful and heartfelt writing.
You never know who you're inspiring."
- Jay

"Her words hit me in my core!"
- Jammy

"Well done the tension, cadence, performance, scenery, and word choice created a piece that oozes that sensual feeling."
- Tyler

"Your voice and your mind are a blessing... seeing your writings and hearing your soothing voice, you inspire me to dig deeper and raise my game. Keep doing what you're doing and you will touch a lot of souls. This is your purpose... Thank you for sharing your gift..."
- Terrence

"Continue to write for those that can't put those healing feelings together."
- Mariel

"I'm soo proud of you in the things you do to empower those around you. You are truly blessed with a special light and you are letting it shine more and more as time goes on and it's soo beautiful to see. You're beautiful to see. But your light shows through from a deep place within you, it's more than skin deep."
- Dee

"You definitely a light in this dark world and I see what you're doing fr and I'm in absolute awe fr."
- Angelo

"Even through text your presence is powerful."
- Gabriel

This book is for every person who has fought
battles they hid from the world ..
wars they begged God to get them through ..
& for those who have succumbed to deep
internal heartaches ..
the kind you bury 6 layers deep into your subconscious ..
just to keep from running away from yourself.

You are enough.
You always were.
& you always will be.

I love you.

xo sabrina

It takes a village.
Thank you to my solid ground – My Family.
My Madre. My Grandparents. My Sisters & Brothers.
My Tios & Tias. My Primas. My Best Friends.
My Extended Family. My Online Community.
& those I have gained through the years.
Thank you for loving me unconditionally;
for never giving up on me & all my impulsive,
wild ideas.

Siempre Loca, Pero Libre.

Para La Niñita Dentro de Mí

~ *Preface* ~

Love is Boundless began on a Sunday in September.. that time of the year where we're all beginning to get giddy with the Halloween spirit, indulging in all things pumpkin spice while it's a scorching 93 degrees outside. Well, at least if you live here in California, hehe! I had decided that on that Sunday, September 23, 2022 - that I was going to experience a healing session accompanied with the healing properties & spiritual enlightenment of psilocybin mushrooms. I had done hella research about shrooms over the last year on how to prepare for a safe session & the best ways to consume these magical plants - so I felt more than ready to receive all the healing & clarity this session would bless me with.

I remember this feeling of a slow, gradual bliss, peace, & overwhelming love cleanse over me as I slowly danced around my room in silky, red lingerie, listening to *"Do 4 Love"* by Snoh Aalegra on repeat for hours. That song has become the anthem of my inspiration in which *Love is Boundless* bloomed from. It all started with a poem I wrote during this healing experience, **THE** *Love is Boundless* poem itself! I had been under an anxious writer's block for almost 6 months - since my Dad had passed away.. & it suddenly began to dissipate as the words about this newfound love I was just now becoming conscious of - began to flow effortlessly from my pen. I had discovered something within me that I had been externally seeking for so long.

This turning point of awareness was a full circle moment in my decade long healing journey of self-love, forgiveness, & acceptance. I felt liberated as I continued to write line for line about a boundless love that would forever leave a lasting impact on my soul. It's really one of my greatest tower moments up to this point because it has shifted my paradigm of thinking on solitude & what it means to love another human being while living consciously within this physical realm. I soon entered what I started to call, my "creative renaissance." I was on fire writing beautiful poetry every day. Somewhere between the heat of my rebirth & creative explosion, this book was envisioned & now, here we are, as it has been brought into fruition!

What was first only going to be a short chapbook containing 31 of my newest poems written during my "creative renaissance" period, is now an intentional collection of my work over the last 10+ years. In this book, I have compiled a total of 204 pieces of my work with 133 of them being poetry. The decision to piece together a collection just felt better aligned in capturing the essence & full embodiment of my book's title. I wanted to share the ranges of love I have fought to find on my path, the growing pains & heartache, & the self-love & romance that I nurtured through the years with healing & forgiveness. *Love is Boundless* is the arch I climbed & the valleys I trekked in search of the greatest love story ever told, the one I had been writing all along & didn't even realize it - ***my own***.

***

This book is divided into several different themes. Each theme contains two sub-sections: one for poetry & another for thought pieces. I decided to break it up this way so that my readers - **YOU** - can decide what you want to read while keeping it simple & cohesive. The themes themselves are also intentionally organized from heartache to healing, love, & everything in between. I decided to put my heartache in the first section so that you may accompany me on this journey of healing & growth. I wanted to share my journey in a way that could show where I was - rock bottom - to where I am now - a place of peace & gratitude (progressing towards the end of the book). It wasn't always this way & thus - the journey of darkness is just as important as the current level of growth & healing that I am at now.

In some of my thought pieces I have provided question boxes for some self-reflection journaling. These are questions that I have asked myself to help me sort through the chaos & build self-trust. These are also questions I use when coaching clients - as my technique is not to just tell you the answers, but rather to give you the support & tools to help you discover them within yourself.

So - that brings me to say - this book is not meant to be read in any particular order, but in any way that calls to you. Whichever section is popping out to you most - is where I encourage you to start. Every section is filled with love, intention, & healing. It is my hope that my experiences - at any point in my life - can remind you how much you are loved, needed, & admired.. even in the darkness of your own solitude or at the peak of your success - **you are worth a boundless love**.

***

Something I went back & forth on while putting all of my pieces into one place - was the grammar & editing. If you have been with me for the last decade & followed my blog - you know I am not a huge perfectionist when it comes to grammar or writing etiquette. That must be the Aquarius in me. I write how I speak, I don't always capitalize or put commas in the right place. Run on sentences are my kryptonite & free flow is more my style. In one of my podcast episodes & possibly on my blog as well - I remember mentioning that I write from a sense of familiarity & comfort. I want my readers to feel like they are just sitting in my living room choppin' it up with me. For me - the message is more important than being grammatically perfect. I do promise though to use *"their, there, they're"* correctly, & to also spell words correctly! Haha! As you go through the different pieces, just know it's **RAW**, it's **REAL**, & it's **ME**. I have my own style, my own rhythm & I didn't want to edit that because it just did not feel authentic to me & who I am as writer. Perfection didn't make the cut this round, just realness.

***

This entire book was such a beautiful experience to piece together. Going through my notes app, my notebooks, & my blog to select the different pieces I wanted to include was *quite* the process! A lot of my work is still not included here in this book, but every piece that is here, was picked with intention. My collection is composed of poetry, conversational responses I gave to other people, small quotes I wrote, & pieces I wrote for social media or my blog. This entire experience has been very challenging, but it also provided me with even more opportunities to heal, grow, & reflect on my life. I am grateful that you are here & have chosen this book for yourself. This book is me wearing my heart on my sleeve. Please treat it with gentle kindness.

Now, the cover! I would have to say the cover was one of my favorite pieces to create. Just as with everything else, there was a lot of intention that went into every aspect of the cover. As I reflected on what *"Love is Boundless"* meant - I knew that I wanted to share its meaning with everyone I knew. I could not keep this profound discovery to myself. The open cage on the cover represents liberation, elevation, & transcendence. It is the breaking of the matrix from oppression, limiting beliefs, trauma bonds, generational curses & societal conditioning. While the rose petals represent love, consciousness, healing, & legacy. How could I discover a boundless love & keep it caged in for myself? How could I elevate, but not sprinkle that frequency amongst others? It is my purpose to leave a trail of rose petals everywhere I go. To embody love so that love is what I radiate. To express love so that others may feel safe enough to express it too. I hope that by the end of your reading experience with me - you can take some of the rose petals & seeds I have sown into these pages & plant them within your own garden.

I hope that whatever it is you are looking for on your life's journey - I hope you find it. I hope you never let it pass you by out of fear or imposter syndrome. I hope you capture it, but never cage it - I hope you share it with the world. I hope you gift us with it.

Bloom, my loves, bloom.

Love is Boundless

September 25, 2022
song: "Do 4 Love" by Snoh Aalegra

It was not the smell of your skin ..
or the taste of your lips ..
it was not the touch of your hands ..
or the thrust of your dick ..
it was never the world-ly feel of your body ..
but the depth in which
 your soul dove inside me.

I never touched you ..
you never touched me ..
but still love was rooted
& decided to blind me ..
but was I really blind?
or was I starting to see
for the very first time?

'Cause you see - pun intended ..
there was something
that you taught me ..
love is boundless ..
& yet still ..
you caught me ..
intertwined your soul within my vines ..
& now roses grow with you in mind.

Follow Your Heart

Intro: What is Love?

When I used to think about love, I thought of it in the way I was conditioned to believe it should be like. I held onto a very rigid expectation that love is supposed to stay confined within these societally constructed boundaries, otherwise it wasn't real. It was a façade & there was no way that person truly loved me. It's often difficult to shift your perspective on what love should look & feel like when you've been stuck within a drastically different paradigm of thinking your entire life. The change is often inspired by an awakening within your consciousness. It's like you are suddenly made aware of your subconscious mind & may feel pushed into a level of awareness that has you questioning every belief, standard, & expectation you hold about love. Some questions you may find yourself asking are:

"What is love?"
"What does it mean to love?"
"How does one give & receive love?"
"Why do I love the way I do?"
"Have I ever experienced love?"

This beginning stage of awakening through a paradigm shift to a true & boundless love can be triggering. It is especially uncomfortable when you fully embrace your curiosity to answer these questions &

discover some rooted traumas &/or experiences that you may not have fully healed from. Taking the time to examine your responses with compassion & patience is the key to learning & unlearning any beliefs around love that you no longer align with.

Every day we are highly stimulated with so much information telling us what is & isn't okay when it comes to love & how we should be loved in return. It can be overwhelming to figure out what you might think is best for YOU when you have a million "love gurus" all over social media telling you what *should* be best for you. I want to take a different approach to discussing love. I want to share my experiences & wisdom in a way that provokes you to reflect & look deep within yourself for the answers you seek. I don't want to tell you HOW to love, rather I want to challenge you to discover that knowledge within your own heart & soul. To uncover the living love inside that fulfills & inspires you to love yourself & others more deeply and unconditionally.

As you proceed through the different sections & themes within this book, remember that everyone's experiences are different, & this is my journey to a **boundless love** being shared with you. May my art spark love & curiosity towards your own **boundless love** discovery.

~ *Heartache: Poetry* ~

My heart hurts ..
it's so heavy w grief & heartache ..
swollen w loneliness.

xo sabrina

4:44am thoughts

January 27, 2022

There are so many words in so many languages ..
yet none of them can fully express ..
the inner heartache that I feel ..
having to accept that I'm single ..
& there's nothing I can do about it ..
it's honestly drowning me on the inside.
I feel like I'm trying to ignore it, but really ..
it haunts me late at night ..
when I crawl in between my cold sheets
w no one to hold me or keep me from falling ..
into the darkness of this fight.

I am forced to be okay in this loneliness ..
I am forced to believe that:
"it's okay what's meant for me will find its way."
but what if I was just honest?
what if I stopped lying & said I'm afraid
I'll never have the love I desire ..
what if I told you that I'm afraid of spending
another decade on my own?
I'm afraid that another year will come & go,
& I'll still be lying in this bed alone.

Telson

March 09, 2021

You seem to be expecting me to write about you ..
So here is what I'd say ..
As a writer..
I'd never put you down ..
Even though we both know ..
I feel some type of way.
I'd never slander or degrade you ..
Break you down to build you up ..
Despite your recent behavior ..
Only forgiveness ..
Flows from my cup.
Years ago I learned ..
It isn't always about me ..
So when you raise your *telson* ..
It's your protection from pain ..
That I see.
To read you is to see you ..
A skill many aren't able to do ..
But I felt you ..
& I feel you ..
So with that, I learned how to.
You can disengage your ego now ..
Lower your stinger from the defense ..
Save your venom for a true villain ..
I hate that things between us got this tense.

to a scorpio.

{9}

She knows

March 03, 2020

I know they say that mercury retrograde
brings about old feelings & wounds ..
Past lovers & memories hidden in our subconscious
brought back to our conscious mind,
surfacing undealt w emotions &
the traumas & triggers that we fear to face ..

It's during this transitional time that
I am hit w a troubling truth ..
a fact within myself ..
that I may be afraid to admit out loud ..
but here I am .. here I go ..

It is w her that I ever felt
what intense connection felt like ..
It is w her that I told all of my darkest truths.
I felt free to be who I was ..
to share who I wanted to become ..
In all my hesitation with anyone else ..
It is w her that I opened up like the
red sea & poured out my soul ..

She could never bore me ..
She could never turn me off ..
but she could upset me haha ..
Oh how irritated she could make me feel ..

Love is Boundless

Our crossing felt timed ..
It felt like it all fell into place just when
I needed her to be there ..
& there she appeared ..
on a friday night .. I saw her ..
One swipe right because instantly
I knew she was exactly who i wanted.

I fell for her.
I loved her.
& that scared me, so I left her.
I feared my own emotions for her.
& in being consumed by my fear ..
I hurt her..

Today ..

The connection still lingers somewhere between us ..
but no longer are we intimately sharing in it ..
Fading ..
Strangers again ..

I think about her all the time ..
what she's doing .. how she is ..
Asking myself if this is how I'm
going to live the rest of my life ..
Loving her w out ever touching her ..
Moving on w someone new ..
Will I still think of you?
Do you still think of me?
I wonder what it could have been ..

(continued next page)

If ..

But I could never say these things out loud ..
I could never admit how much I loved her
& feared that love ..

but I know *she knows* ..
I know *she knows*.

Right click ..
Select all ..
....
Delete.

a response, "I Blame it on the Boogie"

September 21 - October 01, 2022

He grooved his way into my DMs, eager for my attention,
all that alluring & delicious intellect, I let him in - no hesitation,
accepting his offer to dance -
oh how I wish back then I knew what I know now ..
he was pimp steppin' his way into every girl's mentions ..
foolishly my heart agreed to boogie her way into his game,
"Makin' bitches fall & then slippin' away"
claimin' to be fair - it was all 'cause
"I don't wana hurt you, I love you, & for you I deeply care" -
the venom glistening every time he licked his lips ..
in awe, I was encapsulated by his poetical excuses,
followed by his philosophical reasoning - a justified list ..
the drop in his voice, soft & sensual,
making me believe every rhythmic line,
& as he spoke - every syllable vibrating ..
breaching the boundaries of my worn heart ..
as her logic faded w time ..
here I was .. slowly unraveling ..
as my guarded walls fell apart, a gentle burn ..
'cause although painful,
he spoke w an articulated eloquence, a soothing tone ..

I was hypnotized ..
fallin' in love w a nigga over the phone ..
all while his manicured hands held
my bloody, seeping **corazón**,
dripping between his fingers & down his arm,
his silver rings & beaded bracelets
soaked in my rueful vulnerability
as he wooed me w his stealthily charm ..
then .. calmly he returned my whimpering heart to
her cage between my breasts ..
being sure to remind me he would be fine, but for me -
his heart could never be mine ..
"Only to purpose am I attached,
I cannot love you more than I love that .."
I was an experience on his journey,
"research" added to the score ..
just another piece on his board ..
& "checkmate" -
it was now time for his next dance,
dippin' out on me as fast as he had slid thru my IG ..
poetically groovin' his way into the next bad bitch's heart.

In love & art - there is always both light & dark.

karmic soulmate

March 17, 2021

Why do I feel this intense connection ..
it's silent but I know it's there ..
I can feel a pull towards you ..
it's magnetic .. say you don't feel it too ..
intuitively I can sense your resistance ..
you hold back & coldly keep me out ..
but my heart sees right thru it ..
I swear to it .. no doubt ..
& if you've moved on ..
touched her the way you touched me ..
passionately kissed her lips while cumming inside her ..
the way you would kiss & cum in me ..
then I'm delusional ..
& I pray God clears my sight so I can see.
I'm letting you go now ..
I release my hope from this ..
sever the soul ties that bound you to me ..

it hurts ..
it stings ..
only briefly ..

& then ..
I am free.

now I see what it do

October 13, 2022

You told me how our love felt like
we were livin' in a dream ..
I didn't see it then, but now I can agree ..
'cause who you're comin' off as now ..
isn't at all who you seemed ..

But ..

Let me circle back right quick,
I'm not tryna project -
I'm aware enough to know
my perception of you is subjective -
to who you chose to show ..

Maybe you were slackin' in ya mackin'
& fell in love too soon,
lost in a game of charades ..
or maybe I was lackin' in my 20/20 vision,
blurred sight of the real you ..
missin' all ya red flags ..
puttin' your ass on a pedastool ..

Shit was unclear at first,
but now I see what it do.

my heart took an "L"

October 24, 2022

unrequited love ..
so hopeful ..
yet so far ..
I had to stop waiting for your call ..
my heart took an "L" -
but ..
just had to accept that fall.

Empty Eyes

April 02, 2018

Forever searching the empty eyes
of those who enter her body ..
searching for a spark,
a glimmer of hope ..
that maybe this time,
it's more than just sex.

Avoidance

August 29 & September 1, 2022

I don't even know where to start ..
not sure where to begin ..
there's a lump in my throat -
chakras blocked within ..
I've been hesitating lately
& it's very unlike me,
I've been dreading this ..
afraid of what might float to the surface ..
I know I've been avoiding what I'm about to say -
I know I've been tryna put all this pain on delay
& consciously still ..
I went to bed every night ..
telling myself:
"I'll get to it another day."

(A poem about the challenges of facing the sudden death of my estranged father.)

~ Heartache: Thought Pieces ~

Death of an Estranged Parent

May 23, 2022

We don't talk enough about estranged parents who assisted in our childhood abandonment issues & unhealthy attachment styles - passing away. We don't talk about the confusion & mixed emotions you are slammed with when they die & you're left trying to understand the pain you feel.

We don't have enough conversations surrounding the guilt, anger, heartache, & the questions you are overwhelmed w when they are no longer here to heal the bond that was torn in childhood. The suffocating, throat choking realization that you'll never have a relationship w them in this lifetime - especially when that's all you've ever wanted. Well - let me start the conversation. Whatever you are feeling is valid & the confusion is normal. Don't avoid anything that comes up. Sit through it & process all of it. Cry, scream, yell, ask questions, pray, & mourn *your* way. But most of all - don't shame yourself for the decisions you made to protect yourself & your heart when they were alive. Be self-compassionate in knowing you did what you had to do for **YOU**. & You created boundaries that you felt *honored* your sanity & peace.

No one can tell you how you should feel, no one understands the pain you felt as a kid & how you've carried that heartache w you through life, praying one day it'll heal & you'll no longer have to heal from the wounds inflicted on your soul. Only you can feel & know that. & I feel this w you. I'm here in your pain w you.. if you are here in this, I send you my heart.

Be gentle w yourself.

Shade

August 14, 2019

I don't know how to get to know anyone. I don't know how to fall in love in healthy ways. I don't know how to seek through the souls of others w out drowning in the waves of my own self doubt & fears. I don't know what it's like to have someone good – someone who really means what they say. I don't know what honesty sounds like. I couldn't tell you what the truth should feel like. I couldn't even tell you why I question the best of ppl when they have done everything to show me they are safe. I don't know it until it's over, until I've pushed them so far away I can't even hear them anymore. They are no longer listening. My screams of trust issues & past traumas are deafening.. people turn & run – they realize I'm not saveable. It's too late for me. I'm broken, & no cement glue or healing workshop could put me back together the same. I could light endless sage & read a million horoscopes, play positive energy music, & read self help books, & quotes.. but none of that will erase this... nothing will bring me to the light w out any shade.. shade lives inside me.. It's found a home inside of my crushed heart & dances w my damaged soul ... it is afraid of anything too beautiful, it is afraid of anything too good, it is afraid of too much light because it has been deceived before... it's safer in the shade... so to the shade we recede... when the light seems too close.. when happiness is inching itself into my soul again... I catch it, back to the shade we go... it's safer there. **It's safer alone.**

{ 27 }

Starved

June 20, 2020

I'm afraid to be touched I'm afraid to be hugged when I'm sad I don't know what it feels like to be wrapped in the arms of someone who never wants to let go .. I try to remember what it feels like to feel loved .. you know the kind where they can't wait to see you, where I can be myself & not feel judged.. I've never had that..

Always searching always praying wishing on stars that someone will find me & love me foreal this time .. being starved of true intimacy & connection & feeling deathly dehydrated from never feeling understood.. I can't breathe sometimes because it's like i'm dying I need to be touched I need to be hugged & caressed .. I need to be seen, heard, felt ..

I am drowning in the lack of skin to skin contact I never feel .. my stomach is sinking my lungs are shrinking .. my eyes are flowing with the desire to cry but I'm all dried up .. numb to this loneliness & this thirst that is never quenched this swallowing feeling of despair & heartache .. shielding my soul to protect myself of the disappointment & pain .. that maybe life was meant for me to be alone .. maybe these are the cards I was dealt .. because I don't know what it feels like to be wanted .. to be cherished & appreciated.. I never had that before..

I never had that before.

Guilty

May 22, 2019

Honestly it's like I feel so guilty for feeling lonely sometimes, it's like I feel like I'm not thankful enough if I am sad. How can I be so ungrateful? With amazing supportive & understanding friends, loving family who will root for me no matter what I'm doing.. how can I allow myself to feel just the slightest tugging desire that I want a significant other? How can I even act as tho that is worth being sad over.. after all I've been through, after all that I have worked on within myself to heal, to pick up all the shattered pieces of my heart & welding them back together, building a beautiful pattern that is not quite the same as it was before it broke.. how can I just forget the peace I've worked so hard to find.. the contentment in knowing I am enough & I will be accompanied by someone amazing in god's most perfect timing... how can I forget the promises God has spoken into my soul... how can I?

No.. I feel so guilty when I feel alone.. I don't wana cry I don't wana give into my yearning heart ... I don't wana **WANT** anyone.. I want to remain in my peaceful solitude w no questions of when? I don't wana envy those who have the family I want ...

No..

I feel guilty when I'm sad. Because I have an amazing life .... sometimes tho.. being alone all the time can remind you of just how lonely you really are.

Your King Will Spot You

March 30, 2016

It breaks my heart to see so many young women displacing their value into the eyes of selfish & superficial men who lust after their physical attributes and or their monetary investments. It hurts me, it burns me to the core. Why? I silently cry for these broken hearts who just long for a man's love in return.. They will give up their entire **WORLD** to show a man they are down. They will make fools out of themselves to prove they are **THE ONE**. Don't get me wrong, I am not perfect.. I too want to find My King.. But I have learned from experience that I will never have to hurt myself for him to notice me. He will see me & he will be strategic in his gentle approach; knocking down the stone gravel that keeps my heart safe from those who don't deserve it.

Baby girls, please listen to me when I tell you.. He will not change even if you **BEG**. I was young at some point too.. I know what you're going through.. I know how this ends. **BE YOU**.. Your happy **YOU** & **your KING will spot you.**

~ *Healing: Poetry* ~

It's been rainy,
laying low & spending solitude in my thoughts ..
penning my manifestations into ink ..
materializing ..
through all the doubt I have fought.

xo sabrina

the evolution

November 24, 2019

it's a rude awakening ..
to sit w yourself ..
facing all your flaws & toxicity ..
soul – both consciously & subconsciously chained
to your pain because you never healed from your past ..
it's ugly – only at first though, excruciating even ..
vulnerably admitting to your faults ..
but it needs to happen eventually ..
evolve.

xo sabrina
forever sitting w myself

Experience is my muse ..
I pull from my heart -
her past, present & future.

xo sabrina

Pieces of Me

February 14, 2021

Scattered, she finds parts of herself within
every situation she encounters ..
the pain triggers the deeper rooted traumas within ..
the trust she had for herself is diminished ..
as she is once again found with a piece of her missing ..
a piece of her has been traded for emptiness ..

Most nights, the warmth of the wool blankets are enough ..
the house is quiet.. stillness echoes throughout her casita as
she sobs between tears she tried holding in ..
the heater is now blowing into overdrive as the
temperature drops to -8 outside ..
the sound of the fridge cycles causing those dollar tree,
margarita, cactus glasses to rattle like a train track ..
she gasps deeply, trying to catch her breath
& wipes her nose on the blue flannel sheet ..

"I love you God.." she whispers ..

safe.
warm.
alone.

There is a comfort here ..
an assurance in knowing that -
here - she can't be hurt.
ironically, **inconsistency** has always been
a **constant** in her life.. & so it is here, alone,
snuggled beneath that blue flannel comforter,
that she finds the consistency she longs for ..
the consistency of being alone with herself ..
piecing back together all the inner parts & pieces
that she overshared with hands that were not willing
to hold such fragility, softness, & weight ..
the weight of her depth ..
the weight of how her soul demanded
one's higher self & awareness ..
the fragility of her patched heart & forgiving spirit,
the softness of her willingness to
understand another's betrayal..
even if ..
in pieces..
is how she is left.

People pleasing

March 18, 2023

When I discuss my passions
& how I am sharing my gifts w the world -
strangers always seem so impressed w all that I do ..
sometimes I get caught up
& I'm reminded of all that I have overcome
& been through ..
all that has brought me to this point ..
I've never really received much validation
from the people I love
& I guess I got busy trying to
be good enough for all of you ..
that I stopped celebrating myself too ..
the route I've taken has not earned me
any higher level degrees or salaries ..
in my culture - they'd call my dreams "fantasies" ..
I've internalized my lack of traditional education
to believing I had to *"make it"* in my heart's calling
before I ever mention anything to the ones I do it all for ..
I've become accustomed to shrinking below
modest levels amongst the people I love
because their in-acknowledgment of my accomplishments ..
was really ..
only a self-projection ..
that maybe .. it's just me ..
who doesn't believe I'm good enough.

To finally share your truth is painful,
but there is liberation in owning your pain
& expressing it out loud ..
even if the only One you share it with is God ..
because in Him,
healing & love can be found.

xo sabrina

I write

March 11, 2020

I feel like I have to write out the toxins ..
write out the sickness from w in my body ..
exude the virus from deep inside myself through
words I release at the tip of my pen ..
it's like I feel something calling to me:

"Write .. write .. write ..
you will get better if you just write ..
you will become healthy, healed, & well ..
if you write it out ..
sit in the dark ambience of your living room ..
listen to soulful, peaceful, sensual music ..
sit & wait ..
sit & just write ..
even if you don't know what to say .."

Allowing my soul to speak through the waiting ..
I sit here ..
reflecting ..
I close my eyes ..
I stretch across my living room rug..
downward dog.. butterfly ..
skip through songs until I find the beat that speaks to me ..
& then ..
I begin ..

Love is Boundless

I am grateful for this life ..
I am grateful for this freedom ..
that I may sit at home in my peace & safety ..
in my sanctuary .. & I rest ..
that I may be able to sleep off this icky feeling
running a marathon through my body ..
to have the words to describe my pain, & joys ..
to express what others may not be able to voice ..
to have paper & pen to manifest those words
into physical forms of the toxins I hold inside my body ..

I am grateful ..
I am thankful ..
so even if I have nothing to say,
even if i'm unsure of what to write ..

I write ..

because there is no where I feel more free ..
more at peace ..
more love & gratitude ..
than here ..
in my dark living room, dim rope lights,
Erykah Badu bumpin on the low ..
w my heater to keep me warm ..
homemade food to keep me full ..
& hot tea to relax & destress my mind ..

& my pen ..
my pen to free me ..

I write .. I heal ..
through my writing I become well.

Find me smudging w the cleansing smoke of sage
the deepest & darkest parts of my soul ..
while I uncover the light that has been
buried underneath all of the broken
pieces of this little girl's heart.

xo sabrina

I love & admire lyrics that share a story
through poetic words & rhythm..
it's the vulnerability – the rawness –
the ability to spill your heart out –
the pain – & alchemize that into a message ..
that's so fire to me .. that's beautiful ..
that's not easy .. & I appreciate that.

xo sabrina

I am my own counsel

April 10, 2020

I think sometimes I feel guilty when I'm sad because
I've worked so hard to achieve this level of peace ..
I've fought to be this content ..
Despite my past with its traumas & heartbreaks ..
It wasn't some meme or inspirational quote
that broke me open & exposed all my shame ..

No, it was 7 years of prayer ..
7 years of filling voids &
sleeping with all my regrets ..
7 years of rock bottom & a
subconscious filled with "what ifs .."

It was a series of lonely nights that turned
into months & months that turned into years ..

It was wounded egos & bruised friendships ..
Missed birthdays & lifetime milestones
I'll never get back ..
Memories I won't ever be apart of ..
& time I can never rewind ..

7 years.
But still ..

I have more work to do ..
more love to find &
more peace to pursue ..

So ..
I free my soul from all the guilt ..
& some days ..
I allow myself to be sad ..

Because my acceptance to fully
expressing & owning my emotions
is what brought me here ..

It is when I stopped hiding from
what I felt & faced all my fears ..

That's when I began to know peace ..
That's where balance..
& self-happiness..
found me.

Be kind ..
Don't allow anyone to change your heart for the worst.
Be yourself ..
Don't let anyone make you ugly inside.
Stay true ..
Real ones gon' see you.

xo sabrina

Being alone there is no choice but to dig deeper ..
to reflect more ..
to love me in ways I didn't think I could.
Connecting to God – He is showing me a mirror ..
& what it looks like ..
to see me from His perspective.

xo sabrina

series: nightcaps w God.
title: pause

August 01, 2018

August already,
& my summer has been eventful as well as restful.
My gypsy spirit is ready for the next adventure.
You all know that even if I stay a while ..
I eventually get up & go ..
when the lessons are learned & the chapters have been read ..
I continue to believe & have faith in all of the promises God's said.
Geez, what a beautiful mural He is painting ..
the outcome will outshine marvelous.
I'm ready for the next precisely picked palette.
I trust Your steady hand as unknown colors glide off
the bristles of your wooden brush ..
Coloring Your Will into my soul
& filling me w love's motivating passion.
Although broken & pounding ..
my heart is ready for wherever you are drawing me to next.
My spirit is listening asking w out sound,
"Where to, mi Diosito?"

"Still, mi princesa .. STILL."

Keep telling your story ..
Although the pain & trauma is heavy ..
It is through our vulnerability in sharing w others
that someone else may believe in
hope, peace, & healing.

xo sabrina

Please .. I CHOOSE YOU!!

January 8, 2023

Time & time again I am left behind
only to drown myself in my own murky depths ..
In the suffocating acceptance that all I can do is
be okay w not being chosen ..
because you see ..
I've never been anyone's choice ..
I've drenched myself in my own solitude
because it's the only place where consistency won't hide -
from me.
When all my heart craves ..
is someone who wants to take this ride -
w me.
Through this physical projection we have named, "Life."

 I am caught between the waves at high tide,
I'm trying to stay afloat ..
Waves crashing at my throat as I choke,
the oxygen gnawing through my lungs
trying to fight the water that's overflowing this boat ..
I'm sinking gasping for just one more breath ..
My arms flailing in every direction ..
Hands trying to grab at the waves as each molecule
slips just short of my grasp ..
I'm running outta breath ..

My heart is climbing her way up my throat ..
Thumping ..
As if her presence couldn't possibly be known ..
I hear her in my ears,
loud & clear:

> *"I'm tryna save you, please stop aching ..*
> *I'm tryna hold you, please ..*
> *No one's coming it's just me & you ..*
> *I'm tryna save you, but I can't ..*
> *if in your worth you don't believe.*
>
> *Please ..*
> *My over-loving heart that carries scars*
> *from all the risks we've fallen through ..*
> *Don't stop loving, don't stop beating ..*
> *Please ..*
>
> *I CHOOSE YOU!!"*

I have discovered my truth.
I am a diosa.
I am beauty,
I am flawed,
& I am still worthy ..
Whether others appreciate my presence ..
or dare to notice my absence ..
My existence is still magical & absolute.

xo sabrina

~ Healing: Thought Pieces ~

The Ugly Truth About Healing

January 08, 2023

We have to speak more about the realness behind the healing, the pain, the rude awakening, the isolation & realization of facing yourself & your choices. It's not all blooming & peace. A lot of it is bleeding from the thorns & questioning your whole life!

The previous poem, ***"Please .. I CHOOSE YOU!!"*** represents the ugly side of healing & solitude. It's the reality that it's not always sunny & calm waters. It gets gruesome, lonely, & painful.. but I promise if you choose yourself, if you keep grasping at the waves, if you keep your courage to live & to love, if you find something to believe in, something to fight for, something to keep floating towards.. Eventually the tides will begin to fall away, the sun will come out.. & you'll begin to feel okay. This journey of healing is not easy, but embarking on it will liberate you from all the false identities & limiting paradigms you've been holding onto.

Choose it & never stop. It'll be a fight & you'll wana recede back to shore because it's "safer"- more familiar .. but those are **not synonymous.** Choose the dive, choose the unfamiliar. Trust your ability to swim & save yourself. Make a home w in yourself & own every room!

Choose to heal yourself today, for the you tomorrow.

Healing & Accountability

It's crazy when I think about how much has changed in my life the last 8 years. I remember how I felt when I used to think that my life was all planned out. I felt hella stressed. I felt like I was striving to live up to this fantasized expectation on how I believed my life should turn out & how I thought my family wanted me to live. If I didn't then I would be unhappy & a failure. After I got married the expectation to be perfect became worse. I felt this nagging presence of **"doing the right thing"** lingering around me & this energy trickled into my marriage. This was how I measured the expectations I had of my now, **ex**-husband. We were going to do things my way, even if he didn't like it, because my way was the "right" way. My way was the path to a perfect, successful life & it had to go how I pictured in my head. Now, looking back & reflecting on my behavior, the patterns of my dating habits & my heartache, I realize that I was straining for a family that I never had. I was striving for the perfect life you see in movies & the perfect marriage. I wanted to be the perfect woman with the perfect life because I grew up so imperfectly. I was heartbroken before I could love any boy. I was left behind before I could under-stand what rejection was. You know, it's crazy, when you get to this place of **accountability & healing,** you begin to see where seeds were planted. The moments that slowly began to chip at the joy of living & being. The broken, dark places that you know hurt you at the time, but didn't realize are still hurting you as an adult. I came to that place

& it was painful. It was painful to admit that I was a product of my broken family, of a single mother who was physically abused before my eyes, of a young Black father who lived up to society's deadbeat statistics. I knew that the only way to move forward, was to examine myself & accept that this was my **truth**, but it was not my **identity**. It was not my life & I was no longer going to drag this subconscious destructive pain into my future. Healing is scary, it doesn't feel good in the beginning. You have to face yourself w all of your faults & all of your rooted bitterness & anger & say *"It's okay, you can come out now. I love you & we are going to get through this."* You have to let yourself **FEEL** & that's scary.. it sucks! But, dude.. it's so worth it.

Loving myself used to feel impossible. There would be days where I would stand in front of the mirror & I would call myself profanities. I would tell myself how ugly & fat I was. I would say, *"Of course your husband cheats on you, because who could be faithful to an ugly fat bitch like you? How could he NOT want another woman?"* I would scream at myself, blaming me for my husband's infidelity. I hated myself & I prayed that I would die. I wanted God to save me & I begged him to give me strength, because if I didn't die, I didn't believe I could live. There is nothing that breaks my heart more now, then looking back on the Sabrina who felt this way. It brings tears to my eyes that she felt this way about herself. That she didn't realize how beautiful, unique, & amazing she is. She is so, so, so beautiful, & she is such a good friend. Her heart is golden, she is so funny & she is strong. I wish I could hug her now & tell her she's going to be okay. I am just so thankful that God heard every single prayer, because He saved her.

He saved me.

The Power of Celibacy:
Honoring Your Authentic Self

July 18 & October 10, 2022

I know that everyone's experiences are different, but here is my personal story on celibacy and intentional sex. When I was very young I made a promise to myself & to God that I would wait until I was in deep love to have sex (I was tryna be realistic so I didn't promise marriage! LOL) & I did. I was in my first really serious relationship when I had sex for the first time at 16 years old. It was planned out very special & worth the wait. It was an experience I didn't have to feel regretful about because there was a lot of love & honor within that choice to wait for the love that felt right for me.

But, here I am 16 years later, & I am now waiting again for a deep love before having sex again. I'm at a different stage in my life & although I am aware that safe, consensual sex doesn't need to include *love* - I am also more aware - through trial & error, that - **that** narrative doesn't work for me. I have made past decisions that didn't align w my original promise made in middle school, & I soon realized those experiences only brought me heartache & pain. Since 2019 I have come back to that truth & have become very intentional w sex & who I share myself w.

Celibacy is acknowledging that you are sexual, but choosing to honor yourself in a way that feels authentic & right for you in this current szn of your life. It can also be very healing & help w culti-vating a deeper intimacy w self. My celibacy journey has been very

INTENTIONAL. I am **CHOOSING** to pause from physically having sex w someone else - because no matter how fine these men are, how good they sound & look on paper.. I'm intentionally NOT having sex w any of them. my desire for something deeper than a fine ass man w a big D*ck .. is spiritual .. it's soul alignment on the highest frequency. My interest in a man, my casual flirting here & there .. won't change that i'm choosing celibacy .. at the end of the day I know exactly what I want & my sexual impulses do not decide that for me.. until someone loves me & shows me their love through consistent action & intentional soul connecting conversations that causes our love to evolve on a much higher consciousness level.. it will always be surface level for me, & it's not hard when you see how a lot of these men move & think out here.. they can "ima do me" .. but I know they're not the one for me .. & I'm coo w that.

I desire sex, I'm sexual af, but I choose to only engage in a sexually physical relationship that honors what I desire in love & soul union. & that can be an awareness that some may find is difficult to stand in when you're hurting, lonely, & the idea of no sex w people who don't honor your desires fully - could very well mean you won't be getting none for a long ass time.

To be honest i thought this would be harder than it was .. but i think when one begins to focus on their inner healings & building up their spiritual strength .. your body follows that which your mind controls.. it was unintentional at first .. & a few months in .. it became apparent that i was actually being quite intentional.. I was in my journey of inner transformation which called for a deeper connection to my shadow self & in my learning of facing my fears & demons & accepting the calling of my life's destiny .. I came to understand that in order to hold more light within myself .. I needed to detach myself physically from having sex w someone else in order to clear any lingering energies.

I am a firm believer in enjoying sex for pleasure & I believe that safe, consensual sex is powerful. I have had my experience in choosing my "yes" & I have exercised a freedom in choosing my "no. In my 1 year of abstinence my creative side bloomed, my peace of mind was constant, & my self-care routine always came first. I focused on ways I could change not only my life.. but the lives of others..

I experienced a deeper understanding in what it means to stick to your boundaries no matter what & how important it is to align yourself with similar energies in which you wish to constantly live in.

What I truly desire is intimacy.. not only physical but emotional, spiritual, & mental.. I have a hunger for connection outside of the normal realm in which we live daily .. to be passionately vulnerable with another .. but I needed to first discover that passionate vulnerability within myself.

the healing here is tough but so beautiful .. it is worth it. I highly recommend a szn of celibacy to anyone looking to go deeper into their shadow self & find a healing that requires a pure energy & no distractions.

It has been a beautiful journey of spiritual solitude & healing & I know that my fast & sacrifice will be rewarded w so much love, peace, & safety w the right person. Sex is a beautiful & spiritual connection between two energy carrying beings. & I am more aware now how important it is that my energy aligns w that of my next partner & vice versa.

IT'S OKAY TO BE HELLA GROWN & NOT BE HAVING SEX.

Don't feel pressured my loves.

I am extremely comfortable w being alone .. The years of healing it took to reach this peaceful acceptance were heavy & lonely .. but I thank God for being w me everyday so that I wouldn't succumb to my loneliness & jump into unhealthy relationships just to avoid sitting w myself. Everyone is different w their healing process.. I am someone who needed the extra time to really sort through the tangled knots of my childhood before I could be comfortable w investing in someone else. I had to let go of the animosity I carried towards myself & get to know who I was through grace, patience, & compassion. It took a decade of ups & downs trying to figure out what God saw in me that no one - &/or *that I* - didn't see in myself. It was a lot of hard work. A lot of crying, screaming, & questioning my worth.. until little by little I broke through the smoke screen & felt immense love for the little girl within me. I have nurtured *la niñita* dentro de mi & created a casita within myself that we - I- never need to escape or hide from. Anywhere I am - I will always be home. Even alone & on my own, I can find peace & comfort in the extended solitude of my journey. My company is my favorite to keep.

My heart - put back together by God & me.

Divine Intervention

July 21, 2017

Life has really been something else lately, and to properly address the chaos.. I've been pushed towards God in the act of trusting Him in a blindness I was first afraid of. I think when we are faced with the loss of control in life altering situations, we allow these unfortunate circumstances to define and break us. It's almost as though we accept the lie that there is no way out, and if this is really happening, then why do I feel like I'm spiraling down a nasty, vivid, make-believe nightmare into Alice's Wonderland? We've all been there, where rock bottom hits you harder than you've prepared yourself for.. you begin to rehearse all the moves you've made, how did you go wrong, where did your decisions and judgement fail you? You begin to allow anxiety and doubt to cloud your mind, which in turn, defines your attitude each morning.

This past year has been filled with experiences that I was allowing to hold me down because I felt like I was doing the best I could, & if doing my best was producing such failing results, then might as well just live with it, right?

God intervened every time. & every time.... I half listened.

I half listened because I felt like I was walking in God's Will.. I believed that I could fix this... ME. God was allowing me to go broke, get hours cut at all my jobs, to be pressured so tough to the point where getting out of bed seemed like a chore rather than a new opportunity. I was seizing the day with the mindset of someone who gives up because life isn't fair. There are times when you will be put through hardships of loss, financial instability, social isolation and loneliness.. You'll wonder how you fell so deep without noticing the **CAUTION** signs on the way down..

God saw me losing control and intervened. He took away from me that in which I was dependent.. money, destructive love, and perfected self-image. He wasn't going to lose me. I cried, and I cried. I prayed and I prayed. I begged and I begged.

Nothing.

Nothing.

Nothing.

Silence.

Stillness.

I walked into church this past Sunday morning, the street festivals had all the roads blocked off & I begged God to make a way.. because I had to be there. I had to be in church, I waited all week to be there, I needed to be there. I found an alley & sped down the street and came face to face with the men who direct the church parking lot, a sigh of thankfulness & relief washed over me... ***"Thank You God, I made it."***

I listened to the sermon.. on love and compassion.. the guy next to me was wearing a cologne that brought to mind familiar memories. It was unreal. As the preacher prayed out and we gave our offerings, the worship team walked back on stage and began to sing a song that I had never heard before...

Tears ran down my cheeks.... God heard all of my prayers, He heard me when I begged for His help.. when I felt like I couldn't fight this world alone.. when I felt so alone...He heard me when I asked for Him to come save me from the money, the lies, the insecurities, the social isolation... He heard me.. & through words on the slides and through the mouths of the worship team, Matt Maher sings:

"Day after day, night after night
I will remember, You're with me in this fight
Although the battle, it rages on
The war is already won .....
And when I feel like I'm all alone
Your love defends me, Your love defends me"

God is continuing to walk with me & bless me. I am still working through letting go & letting God handle all of my struggles, but He is blessing my life with steps of courage, with faith, and the confidence to step up to the plate when things get tough! I am able to see a new day, learn from my past mistakes, and look forward to a promising future with God by my side. I was allowing my anxiety, depression, and insecurities define me, form an identity that was not given to me by God.. God decided that He wasn't going to allow anyone to save me.. not even myself.. I have to RELY SOLELY ON THE LORD... HE IS THE ONLY WAY... as my best friend Ruthie texted me:

"GOD LOVED ME WITH ALL MY FLAWS, HE NEVER QUESTIONED ME, GOD NEVER THOUGHT THERE WAS SOMETHING OR SOME-ONE BETTER OUT THERE. HE WANTED ME."

Money will disappear, jobs will lay you off & cut your hours, cars will stop on you, friends/family/lovers will give up & walk out on you without explanation..... but God will **REMAIN**.

That makes my heart dance and my face smile. I am so thankful. So grateful. God is my **HOPE**.

Jesus intervened.

"Your Love Defends Me" — Matt Maher

While typing this I listened to: "Strong Tower" –Kutlass

"You are my strong tower fortress when I'm weak..."

I think the moment I decided that enough was enough, was more like the moment I was willing to **accept** that it was enough. Through years of emotional abuse, toxic cycles, & constant lying, I never really felt like I could go on without him .. There was this sense of shame & fear about leaving to be alone .. to have to face the world with my failed marriage & everyone yelling *"I told ya so"*
Cause I mean that's what they told me .. what they told us.
There is life after divorce.
There is life after breakups & failed relationships.
There is life after toxicity & abuse ..
I can't promise it's easy.. but I pinky promise,
it's worth the battle to be free & emotionally well.

xo sabrina

Facing you

July 05, 2017

Lately, as I have been trying to make sense of the situation I find myself in... I find that I am remaining calm in a way in which I have not done before.. Of course, words have been exchanged... questions are repeated & some left unanswered.. texts have gone ignored & hurtful actions have been overlooked... silently swept under the rug to protect everyone's ego...

There is a driving force inside of me that feels the need to protect your heart & love you with all of mine.. to be patient & understanding of your flaws, insecurities, & doubts.... to show you what unconditional love looks & feels like... to share with you all of that in which you have always thought you had... until you realized... that you didn't..

In decision to love you... I discovered my own demons.. you broke me open, asked me questions that filled my throat with a lump hard to swallow... you brought me face to face with my own addictions & bad habits.. you watched me as I became more vulnerable & the filtered image of perfection began to chip & rust away.. you told me to let go.. to trust you.. not to be afraid because you never wanted someone perfect.. you wanted someone real... & in being real ... I was challenged to be real with myself.

I began to realize that in choice of loving you.. means beginning to really love myself... you see in me the woman that is broken.. the woman who gives & gives without ever giving to herself.. the lover who surrenders all while sacrificing herself in the process.

I put you on a pedestal.. while I hopelessly prayed at your feet.

You corrected me.

I was to be next to you.. not beneath you. I was to love me before I love you. You wanted to be a team together.. two visions... one goal... two minds.. one heart.

How could I be the best woman for you, if I wasn't even the best woman for myself?

Yet.. no man has ever taken time to see me through... to support me & invest in me. You saw bruising.. but knew I could be healed. You understood that life happens, & sometimes we lose ourselves to our circumstances & situations.. but still... you believe in me.

You aren't perfect either.. I have battled this fall of being in love with a man who has been through similar situations & hurts as I have.. to break down your walls, & gain your trust.. to be supportive & open... to listen without opinion.. it has been hard.. it has been quite a battle...but I too.. believe in you.

Deep in my soul... as I pray to God for His Will to be done... I know that if anything... if not a forever type of love... is to come out of our relationship.. it's that — *while facing you .. I faced myself.*

.... & that is a timeless gift.. in which I will be thankful for......
forever.

Love, Loss, & Growth in "Brew City"

October 11, 2019

Milwaukee.. honestly the memories associated with that city bring me a mixture of extremely opposing emotions/perspectives. First, I think of pain & loss. & then immediately I am flooded with thoughts of love & growth....& that fills me w *gratitude*. Blessed to have been broken down & lost to now whole, standing & found... blessed to have moved away w a heart full of bliss & hope for the unknown. Blessed that I experienced the power of the Lord in my life & the beauty He created out of a mess I was unable to clean up myself. But what I am most grateful for are the ones I now hold friendships with – people I had no idea existed before my chapter in *"Brew City."* Amigas & Amigos who became my only family during lonely holidays & birthdays, during cold winters & hot summers... the *Amigas* who hugged me when the tears wouldn't stop, or who celebrated with me when I accomplished the goals I set up for myself. The *chicas* who spent days & nights trying to teach me *Puerto Rican slang* & how to dance *bachata* in their living rooms at 3am.. the *girls* who introduced me to hood-trap music & what it felt like to own my black girl magic. My Girls. My Besties. The Family I chose for myself – or maybe the ones God chose for me before we even knew our names, because bonds that transparent & unconditional couldn't be anything less than a godsend.

When I share the fact of me being divorced – the response is usually always the same – *"OMG YOU WERE MARRIED?! HOW OLD ARE YOU?!"* & it makes me laugh because I think to myself *"Yo foreal, how OLD AM I?!"* It's like I was married in another lifetime because I'm out here pushing 30 & look & feel like I should still be 22 haha – but so much happened in those almost 6 years of my Milwaukee chapter.. & although the situation with my ex husband ended dramatically & painfully – it's something that I will never regret.

I have honestly never formally written about my marriage experience because it is a part of me that carries a lot of darkness, & as I have become older – I have come to the peace of –*"some things are better left unsaid."* I do not wish to slander & run my ex-husband's name through the mud – for the respect I have for his family & son.

We were both so young – & we both did some awful things to one another. It always stumps me – the process in which strangers become friends – lovers – enemies & then strangers again. From fantasy & wishful thinking at 17-18 years old, to meeting one another for the first time at 20 years old, & him proposing to me in the Milwaukee Mitchell Airport a few days later.. it was like this crazy love story of risks & *"who cares what our family says, let's just do this!"* At some point we had *love & loyalty* for one another – best friends. But people change, circumstances shift, & we grew apart. The love & loyalty we once had for one another turned to *regret & anger*. Somewhere during those 3-4 years.. we lost respect for one another – both harming each other w words & actions that could never be erased.

I will not act as though I am defending what he did to me because he surely broke my heart – but I also know that I did some things that may be unforgivable in his eyes too. Still, in spite of all the damage each inflicted on the other – love will always overcome. God's love & plans for our irrevocably broken marriage would not be in vain. We both needed what we had in order to now appreciate what each of us has today. Divorced & strangers – we learned how to love – even though it is not a love shared between each other- we taught one another that breaking up isn't the end of the world, & yes, it felt like it was when we did... & through that experience I found my way back to my family, to my friends, to God.. **to MYSELF**.

God wiped my tears & kissed all the pieces of my shattered heart... He showed me how all of this led me to my purpose. Led me to the women who need proof that there is life after pain, after separation, breakups & divorce – through the depression & defeat... you **WILL BE OKAY**. Follow your dreams, accomplish your goals & give back to this world with all the pain & suffering you got – & the next time you look up – it will be when you are feeling your most whole, genuinely happy self – & **love will find you.** Right there – healing & living your best life. Smile– & **let God** babygirl...

God always had bigger plans for me – & I see it now. & for that – *I* forgave him. I forgave my ex-husband for all that happened between us – because I could never hold myself emotionally hostage for someone who was never divinely designed for me in the first place.

You were a chapter of mine on love, loss & growth in this beautiful life – & I have a whole book left to write.

As we progress through our healing journey,
we may find ourselves disconnected from some of the people we
love. We may have to find acceptance in creating
our own soul families out in the world because sometimes
the family we are given by blood, is no longer going to
always fully understand & support us in the ways we need them to.

xo sabrina

Setting Boundaries

May 09, 2020

A lot of us carry this burden of feeling obligated to accept the toxic behaviors & negative energy radiating off of the people we love. We feel this heavy sense of guilt looming over us when we find ourselves realizing that we don't want to always be around them. Or when we decide to cut that visit short because anxiety is really starting to trigger. Sometimes the negative energy is too real & for our own sanity .. we need a break. There are times when we just can't always be there for everyone during their toughest moments because we are dealing w our own heavy burdens & healing from our own traumas. I just want to let you know:

It's okay to grant ourselves **S P A C E**.
It's okay to say "**NO.**"
It's okay to leave messages on "**READ.**"
It's okay to **SET BOUNDARIES**.
& It is okay to detach yourself from anyone who
refuses to **RESPECT** those boundaries.

FOCUS ON YOU BABY & protect your well-being at all costs.

When we decide to embrace our struggles, obstacles, & mishaps - we are acknowledging that they do not define us nor do they stop our journey. We have the choice to soak in the rain or dance in it.
So cliché, but if you choose to dance in it, you'll find perspective in realizing nothing can hold power over you - it is **you** who decides your reaction. Embrace the rain, dance in it, & trust that even through the storms, God is always there to dance w you. Your Roses need water to bloom my love, too much sun would wither & dry up those beautiful rose petals.

xo sabrina

Toxic Positivity

September 09, 2021

One thing I do with both friends, family & in my coaching with clients is: **I KEEP IT REAL.** I won't sell you false hope, or tell you what you want to hear just to temporarily make you feel better. What I will do is help you get to the root of your feelings. I will ask you questions about your feelings within the situation that will provoke self reflection & help you to rationalize what you are feeling so that you can be emotionally aware & put things into perspective from a logical standpoint rather than an emotionally fueled one. This is how we begin to reframe our thoughts, rewire our neuro pathways, & begin to be able to control our emotions in a healthy & grounded way that is not avoidant or dismissive like toxic positivity.

I really dislike toxic positivity & how some people are constantly try to force it onto others when life is bogus as fuck at times. I have learned that being positive doesn't mean dismissing that some shit hurts & some shit sucks - sometimes life is chaotic & unfair & it's okay to admit that. When someone is feeling a way - don't try to rush them to "get over it" by using toxic positivity & smothering them w all of these affirmations & avoidance tactics. We need to stop dismissing reality. Instead we need to pause & listen. Listen to their feelings, allow them grace & space to process & reflect. It Is **OKAY** to feel & sit in your feelings for a little while. Nobody wants to sit in it & learn **THROUGH IT** & that's why we got all these emotionally unaware, unavailable, unhealed people walking around with all these trauma wounds - because everybody tryna RUSH through shit w all these: *"but it is what it is i gotta get over it"* avoidance type paradigms when it comes to handling uncomfortable emotions.

Na, we gotta feel & reflect through it! Keep it real w yourself & others - let people feel whatever it is they feel & just be there for them w out throwing in some cliché mantra to bandage the situation. We just can't dwell & drown in those feelings. We have to find ways to live through the unfairness, pain, & losses of life & keep it movin'.. keep growing.

When facing difficult situations we gotta take things one moment or one day at a time. Sort through your feelings & work on grounding yourself in knowing that this situation isn't life or death (unless it actually is - in which this doesn't pertain to you). You will live through that breakup, divorce, separation.. etc.. even if you are alone. You are not in any danger. It sounds silly, but we have to retrain our nervous system to recognize moments of immediate danger & moments that are not actually dangerous - we are only responding to anxious thoughts in our heads that are not actually life or death. It's hard, but one day at a time. Things may be hard & they may not be okay for a while, but you will survive if he/she leaves. You will be okay one day in the future w out him/her. Maybe not today, but one day.

Now, take a deep breath & rest.

I love you.

Solitude is Healing

Sometimes mainstream society can at times associate solitude with negative feelings. But solitude can be a very positive & healing experience when used with intention & wrapped in loving yourself during this current szn. Solitude can be used as an opportunity to reflect on your life, your goals, & your aspirations. It can also help you become more self-aware leading to a blooming of personal growth, self-created happiness, & emotional fulfillment.

An important life lesson I am still learning to embrace is that solitude shouldn't be pursued at the expense of everything/everyone else - aka unhealthy isolation as a fearful protective mechanism. While it's crucial to take time for ourselves, it's equally just as important to maintain & nurture healthy platonic relationships as well. Healthy partnerships - both platonic (family, friends, & networking, etc.) & romantic - are essential in the healing process - as we can also see ourselves through the mirrors others hold up to us. This is both necessary & supportive to one's personal growth & development.

When it comes do romantic relationships - it is important that individuals share a similar vision & are aligned in values. They can work together to achieve their individual goals, while also supporting each other along the way. Emotional maturity, as well as security within a relationship, are key factors that enable individuals to pursue personal growth while also enjoying the benefits of a healthy partnership. Don't be afraid to take some time for yourself while forming meaningful connections with others. Finding a balance between solitude & healthy relationships is vital to blooming to our fullest potential.

If you're afraid of being alone that feeling is absolutely normal. We live in a technological era where we are the most accessible, yet the least humanly connected. One way to work through this fear of being alone is to explore it further & try to identify any negative associations & paradigms you carry about what it means to be alone in solitude.

Have there been situations where solitude didn't go well?
Are there memories that bring up feelings of fear?
Were you ever (forced to be) alone as a child, which may have created
feelings of not feeling safe, abandoned, or neglected?

While being alone can seem daunting, it can also be liberating – offering empowerment, independence, & freedom. Embrace the beauty of your szn in solitude & the unique opportunities it presents you with to grow. Don't feel pressured to jump into the dating scene just because your friends or society says so. Take intentional time to heal & practice being by yourself. This will allow you to focus on your inner growth & learn to be content with your own company. Remember that healing is a lifelong process, & some szns are reserved for just you & God. Through solitude, you can do the necessary introspective work & prepare yourself to be open to receive the kind of love you hope for.

While we can never be perfect, we can work towards becoming our highest selves during periods of singleness, so that we are better equipped to navigate our next season of companionship & pursuing a greater purpose in love that is much higher than ourselves.

I don't think people understand how crucial it was / is for me to not go on a single date this entire year. For me not to commit to a single soul & completely be unattached to any man. It was so crucial that **the lives of so many women depended on it.** I did this as part of a bigger picture God has for me. To be a testimony to other women struggling w their healing process. Struggling w letting go & letting GOD. This wasn't only about me. Naa... a lot of people won't under-stand 'cause most people aren't willing to be alone.. soaking in your pain until your heart swells.

I am so committed to myself & my purpose.
I refuse to be distracted.

Taking Accountability

July 5, 2023

Taking accountability requires you to be honest w yourself. Sometimes we can choose to focus on being a victim rather than reflecting & accepting accountability for our own actions that brought certain experiences & circumstances into our lives. At some point we have to stop turning the other cheek to our own poor choices & accept that the problem has nothing to do w anyone outside of ourselves & everything to do w our own lack of accountability to change & choose healing. Our pain is not justification or an excuse to behave in ways that continue to put us in situations of questionable character that hurts others or ourselves. The journey will have trials & tribulations - but not everything is a test sent from the Divine - some shit you put yourself through & until you get real w you & what you're doing to make YOUR life difficult - you'll continue to find people to blame & external reasons to justify why you're always the victim within the life only you hold the power to create.

This does not apply to situations of abuse & domestic violence. Abuse is never the fault of the victim.

Healing is a Choice & Personal Responsibility

February 24, 2020

If we continue to commit the actions that brought us to the lives we are not happy w.. how can we expect a change or shift? We need to own our faults & actually put effort into that shift. Shifts don't happen w out pressure - apply pressure. Do the work & make the effort to really change & heal. Our friends, coworkers, family, etc cannot do this for us. They are not accountable to our healing or our lives - we are only accountable for ourselves. Making others feel guilty about why you can't change is a form of manipulation. We must stop passively manipulating the ones around us who have chosen to take space away from us because they do not see a change. We must sit in our choices & do something about making better choices.

Life will never be perfect, but you can shift your mindset & per-spective in order to find peace – the work is from within – & **ONLY YOU CAN DO THAT WORK.** We can sit here day & night preaching wisdom & inspirational stories of victory, but unless we actually do the action of working towards changing & healing – we will continue to remain the same.

IT IS YOU & ONLY YOU WHO IS IN CONTROL OF THIS CHOICE.

You deserve a love that doesn't stress you, but only you can decide when enough is enough. Only you can choose how you will spend this short lifetime that we are given. I know that we are all ready for things in our own timing & I know walking away isn't easy. But what-ever happens, you are *CAPABLE* of a life by yourself. You will be okay if you walk away to start a life of your own. Just know, the people who truly care for you, will still love you, no matter what you choose.

xo sabrina

The Power of Shadow Work through Journaling

Shadow work is a challenging process that requires vulnerability & honesty. By exploring our past, even as far back as our childhood, we can work through past traumas & free ourselves from their grasp. Although difficult, I have found that confronting the past has been a liberating & very healing experience. It's like this heavy weight has been lifted from my chest.

The healing process can be both triggering & arduous, but it's important to allow yourself grace & compassion as it is a lifelong journey. You may feel as though you've made progress, & then something happens slinging you back 5 steps & now you realize there's more work to be done. However, by being honest with ourselves & confronting our emotions head-on, we can find work towards gaining clarity & peace. It's extremely vital to acknowledge the parts of yourself that you may not like or want to admit exist. Once you acknowledge those areas within yourself, you can begin the work of embracing yourself in all your entirety.

Something that has helped me so much while on this healing journey is journaling. Journaling is a powerful tool that can help w sorting & identifying your feelings. It is also a great reminder in reflecting on how much you've overcome. By writing letters to yourself, you can practice self love - write/talk to yourself like you do the people you love - you gotta be your own counsel & hype woman/man - always!

As a writer who has been journaling for years, it can be terrifying to face the depths of your own subconscious. But, let my life be a tangible testimony in its usefulness toward growth. The freedom & sense of empowerment that comes with confronting your fears is unparalleled. With each journaling session, you'll build trust within yourself & be able to delve deeper into your psyche.

Remember, your journal is a safe space. You don't have to share the details of your intimate sessions w anyone if you don't want to. By starting with the surface level stuff, you can gradually work your way up to the deeper, more profound truths. You are capable of overcoming anything you set your mind to. **I believe in you.**

If you are unsure on where to start with your shadow work, you can start by exploring feelings that arise during moments of trigger, or you can simply begin a session without any triggers by asking & reflecting on the following questions:

- What am I feeling? Anger? Sadness? Disappointment? etc.
- What about the situation is bringing up this feeling?
- Why do I feel this way about the situation?
- Does this situation feel familiar to me?
- Have I experienced this situation before in a different context?
- Is there fear here?
- Why do I feel afraid?
- When this happened before, how did I handle it?
- Am I upset at myself?
- Do I trust myself? Do I trust the other person(s) involved?
- I can only control me & how I react/handle things - what in this situation can I control?
- What in this situation is out of my control?
- Is this something I can let go?
- Have I communicated my feelings/thoughts/expectations with others involved?
- Did I set expectations without effectively communicating my needs to others?

I am an embodiment of divine feminine energy & light. People have told me I'm hella feminine .. & that when they are around me it makes them want to be more feminine too.. Of course this is somewhat subjective. However, the divine feminine does have some distinct differences from the divine masculine. I always think it's interesting when different people tell me this because I never really thought that about myself. It has been a journey in awakening my true femininity.. to trust myself & what I feel. To just allow myself the space to just be in the midst of all the chaos & remain still. I think it's beautiful & an honor, that while embracing my own femininity I have inspired other women to do the same. It's dope because we need more of this divinity & softness in the world.

I am forever bold, but soft.

xo sabrina

~ Self-Love: Poetry ~

Self-love is the romance
& healing is the dance.

xo sabrina

My greatest challenge has never been
on how to love someone else..
My heart has always been eager to love outside of me.
Naa, my greatest challenge & hardest lesson
has been on how to **unconditionally** love myself.
It's also one of my greatest victories.

xo sabrina

loved into delusion

November 12, 2022

I have been loved into delusion! the good kind -
this love got me being more me than I have ever been!
I feel no fear into hiding or downplaying myself..
Yes, I am **ALL** this!
No, I do not fit into any of the algorithm
niches y'all commit to ..
I could never narrow me down like that.

Most of the time ..
Beauty is too beautiful to be captured
by the lens of a camera or the eyes of others ..
Remember that the next time you find yourself
comparing your beauty to another's.

xo sabrina

Bullied

September 29, 2022

I know what it's like to doubt yourself ..
I know how it feels to look in the mirror
& whisper, *"You're so ugly."*

To question your beauty & doubt your worth ..
To constantly compare your hair to hers ..
To wish your eyes were an emerald green
instead of a coffee brown.
To wish your hips weren't so wide in that red gown ..
I know what it feels like to be the odd one out,
to be humiliated in front of a crowd.

I look back now & remember those days,
it makes my heart ache because back then it felt
like more than just a self-hate phase.
I was conditioned to amplify all my flaws,
& feel unworthy - if unlike other girls - I wasn't small.

I tried to perm my curls to keep 'em straight ..
& pop contacts in to change the color of my eyes ..
I wanted to be anything **BUT** me,
it took years for all that hate to flee.

But now if I could,
I'd wrap little baby me in my arms
& yell how beautiful she is out loud
I'd play with her kinky curls
& compliment her gorgeous brown eyes.
I'd make her feel seen ..
Admire her flaws for all the beauty that she radiates
in every smile, dimple, & unwanted crease.

I know if younger me could visit me now,
she'd see the beauty that I see.

multi-passionate

December 06, 2022

I wanted to fit into a box ..
I tried climbing in,
but I felt claustrophobic ..
limited, anxious, restricted ..
I broke the box down ..
I realized I was still worthy even
w out narrowing down my passions ..
my message is still important even if it takes longer
to find the audience it's meant for ..
I don't have to be one specific way to be loved ..
I can be every aspect of myself ..
dark & light,
conscious & still awakening,
learning & unlearning,
sexy/horny & standing in my sexual boundaries ..
I do not need to tone down or suppress any part of myself ..
I am both a masterpiece & a work in progress,
& can still be taken seriously,
can still be heard, loved, & appreciated ..
brains & beauty ..
all of it I embody ..
my ambitious goals do not change
my soft & nurturing heart ..

I do not need to choose between the
multi-dimensional aspects of myself ..
I can just be me ..
& now that i have accepted that all
these truths can be simultaneously true ..
I'm so free ..
I'm basking in self-recognition & acceptance ..
I am released from who the world decided I should be ..
& this brings me so much peace.

I will never water down me -
my intensity to be deep ..
even in the shallowest of moments ..
to satisfy nor impress you.

xo sabrina

A letter to la chiquilla morenita dentro de mi

February 06, 2023

I hope I've made you proud,
I hope the life I've worked hard on creating for us
is a reminder of how much you are valued
& appreciated.
You are beautiful no matter the weight
on the scale or the contoured makeup on your face.
Your love for others is as deep as the galaxy
& no matter where I go ..
you'll always have a home within me.
Today we're 33 ..
& I'm so grateful for the old age
our body has been blessed to see.
Keep being kind, keep being goofy & sweet.
You are loved by the woman you've grown to be ..
ME.

if magic were in tears

November 18, 2022

If magic were in tears ..
I'd have an endless supply of power
from all the crying over the years ..
if beauty was felt rather than seen ..
then maybe my soul wouldn't have gone to
all the heartless pits of men in which I have been ..
seeking refuge amongst liars & sin ..
but..
tears carry no magic,
only pain in which my soul is cleansed ..
& beauty is recognized through
the eyes of shallow men ..
so I no longer pray for love from others
because my heart has seen ..
on this world - my purity could never depend ..
I embrace my indifference
& have chosen to accept ..
if there is no soul here to love me
the way in which I ache to be loved ..
at least I know ..
I chose to love myself
& continued to radiate my
soul's true kindness of touch ..
even on the days I really ..
just wanted to give up.

To have full faith within myself
to make anything happen ..
To know I can depend on me ..
To know I will take risks for myself
time & time again ..
To know I will never stop
myself from dreaming
& going hard for me..
This a top tier love story.

xo sabrina

loving me

November 17, 2022

I've started this over 2x already ..
because I'm just not sure what to say
or even where to start ..
should I focus on my curves?
or my big beautiful heart?
should I tell the world about my pain,
or skip right to the good parts?
if I were writing about the man that I love ..
it wouldn't even feel this hard ..
so why is writing about loving me
got me overthinking on where to begin?
like a novice writer I'm blocked ..
the words forcing themselves
to stumble from within ..
like a jammed printer
I'm trying to yank them out ..
it's so much easier to describe
the love outside of me
but describing my good qualities
has me feeling guilty ..

to talk about my beautiful soul
& curvaceous body has me
wondering if all they'll read is "EGO" -
but I know this is exactly why I have to do this ..
to overcome this guilt of loving me
& all the beautiful things that I embody ..
I have to let go of this fear that
choosing to focus on me
won't have me missing anything
or anyone meant to love me ..
I can love you & I can love them ..
I can love us while simultaneously
always loving me -
loudly & unapologetically.

deep b*tch

July 5, 2023

I'ma deep b*tch.
mentally stimulating,
always observing & analyzing ..
intellectually captivating,
spiritually elevated ..
deep b*tch.
& that's not up for silencing ..
go choke on your simple minded,
people pleasing,
mediocrity ..
or whatever that one meme said.

Coming home to my safe space of
love, peace, & solitude ..
Throwing on some sexy red lingerie
to cook for myself ..
Playing slow jamz while I sing
& dance around my tiny kitchen ..
Grateful is an understatement ..
I prayed, manifested, & fought to be here ..
Truly a journey it has been ..
but I'm here now ..
& I'm in love w all of this.

xo sabrina

Embrace aging.
There are so many people who didn't
& won't make it to the age you're at.
Celebrate each year w gratitude.
Be proud of the years you carry.
It's truly an underestimated
blessing & honor to grow old.

xo sabrina

The real flex is enjoying your own company
& overcoming your codependent attachment
in needing to be w people at
all times to avoid your feelings,
your pain, your truth.
Once you've faced your own darkness ..
there is nothing that can scare you.
Not even loneliness.

xo sabrina

dear chica

August 03, 2021

Dear Chica,

If you are struggling to see your own beauty & radiance,
let me say that your soul is shining through,
your heart is glowing & although you wonder
if you're as beautiful as all the others...
I want to AFFIRM:

YOU ARE STUNNING QUEEN.
& I SEE YOU!
YOUR DELICATE WINGS UNIQUELY PATTERNED
IN A LOVE SO VIBRANT & BOLD –

Keep gracefully gliding along the warm summer breeze ..
like a butterfly –
Seeing you stretches a smile across my face ..
To witness you –
even if just for a moment ..
A tiny glimpse ..
is more beauty than even a moment could possibly carry
& anyone would be blessed to experience it.

xo sabrina

Was I too soft?

July 06, 2021

Was I too soft? Or was the world too hard?
Like the pillows you dream on or the clouds above your head ..
How about that gentle breeze that brushes
against your cheek on a hot July day ..
Do you see it? Can you feel it? Close your eyes & sit in it ..

Was I too soft? Too gentle or too kind?
"How do you keep loving after all that you've been thru?
The way they all treat you? Girl, I admire you.."
Maybe it was the trauma, the childhood pain,
the heartbreaks & loneliness ..

Or maybe I'm just soft ..
A soul connected to light & love ..
Peace & calm ..

Or maybe .. just maybe ..

The world is too hard ..
& softness is how I change it,
a legacy to **BECOME**.

One thing about me -
no matter what szn I'm growin' thru ..
I'ma always date myself.

xo sabrina

When you know better,
it's the self-accountability -
that makes you choose better.

xo sabrina

freedom

May 27, 2021

I am most free on the road,
w the wind in my hair,
the sun in my eyes,
shuffle on my playlist
& the speakers on loud ..
a free spirit always ready to fly,
gracefully transcending –
not afraid of leaving the unaligned behind,
grateful despite the adversity I've faced,
for every battle I fight ..
is worth these dreams I chase.

Some feel that they have
nothing to offer me because
I don't need SAVING.
I SAVED MYSELF.

xo sabrina

~ Self-Love: Thought Pieces ~

Your life is a reflection of how much you love yourself,
how much you mean to you.
What does your life look like?
Are you looking out for you?
Or are you your own roadblock?
Are you the reason you aren't where you wana be?
How can you show up for yourself that
promotes your growth & happiness?
What can you start doing or working on
today that will elevate your life
& begin to reflect that **YOU LOVE YOU?**

xo sabrina

In the past I was never treated like a princess.. I settled because I thought that's all I could get.. I overextended myself for men who didn't do the same for me.. I was a sweetheart to people who didn't value the love I excitedly shared.. I have come such a long way.. & I have healed so much inner hate within myself .. I have dissolved feelings of unworthiness & I have wrapped myself in a love so pure from within myself.. I stopped settling & I started choosing. But it all started with me, w being honest w myself about what I was allowing & why. I began to treat myself like a princess.. Dating myself, showering myself w the romance I desired.. I know now that I deserve the world .. & one of these days God is going to surprise me w a man who wants to give it to me.

'Til then, I'ma give it to myself.

Finding My Sexy

September 16, 2021

I've practiced celibacy & been single for years - & just recently I learned the importance of *"not saving your sexy for someone else."* I started sleeping in lingerie as my norm every night even though my bed has known none other than my own company. Sexy isn't something validated from others - it's how you **FEEL** about yourself. I used to always feel like I wasn't "sexy" because I wasn't "womanly." I felt like my baby face, chubby curves & not so "adult" looking body wasn't sexy. I was looking for sexy in others & trying to replicate that - & that's not *itttt!* Sexy is subjective! Fostering self-acceptance, self-love, & building up my self-esteem & confidence is how I found my sexy & I began to do things that made me *feeeel* sexy even if no one but me got to see or experience it.

I have lived in many places, in many cities in four different states.. but I have always made my spaces feel like home & fill them w so much love because home should feel like your safe space. A sanctuary of peace. I can start over & over again from scratch a million times.. It's not the material things that make a home a home, but the energy within it.. Being intentional w my space is why I enjoy every home I've ever lived in. I do not allow negativity to taint the vibes of my *casita*.. Creativity flows because I feel safe & yet fully embraced by the love I pour into my environment.. By expressing gratitude every time I leave & arrive home.. By cleaning & taking care of my space no matter how big or small.. & Also by pouring into myself.. That is the real reason I can go & live anywhere .. because I have created a home *dentro de mi* .. & that's all I really need.

Never Settle, Keep Going

April 20, 2020

Initially, when we first begin a goal or chase a dream, we are always full of excitement & motivation.. Our dreams of promise & hope seem MORE than reachable.. We are on FIRE! We begin the journey to be & do all it is we desire – the passion is electrifying. Then .. everything slows down.. the challenges to be greater become tougher .. The motivation dies out & inspiration becomes harder to find .. We find ourselves wrapped up in the self-doubt, in the searching of all the promise & hope we started w .. trying to magnify the little enthusiasm we have left .. This is where **THE GREATEST** separate themselves from those who give up.

- Are you giving up on what sets your heart on FIRE because of the time it's taking, the finance it's costing, or the work it requires?

- Why settle & allow all the odds to stack up & defeat you?

Time will continue to move forward so ..

- Why give up only to use your time on something your soul doesn't sing for?

Naa, **BE THE GREATEST!** Life is rushing past us .. Might as well make the rush worth your while!

Romance Ya Own Life

Life is too short to miss out on beautiful experiences just because you don't have someone to enjoy them with.

Why wait for others to fulfill your dreams?
Why not go out there and give yourself the world?

Start small, like going to the movies or dining out alone. Then, slowly work your way up to bigger adventures like concerts, amusement parks, & even traveling solo. Don't be afraid to step out of your comfort zone, because that's where growth, healing, & love can be found. There is empowerment & liberation in doing things alone, so seize the moment & embrace the journey. Imagine laying on your deathbed & regretting not doing what you wanted because no one wanted to go w you! So, get off your booty & start living your life to the fullest! Here are some ideas to help you get started:

- Always keep fresh flowers
- Go on picnics and take naps
- Visit drive-in movies, concerts, and festivals
- Dine at fancy restaurants and take road trips
- Take cozy nights in with candles and watch shows/movies
- Deep condition your hair and stargaze

- Take nature walks, visit museums and art shows
- Perform full moon rituals
- Buy your favorite fruits and cook your favorite dishes
- Visit comedy clubs and stay open to new experiences

Don't wait on others to fulfill your void & complete your bucket list. Don't let societal "norms" hold you back. Be the master of your own ship, & let your soul guide you.

The only life you'll regret, is the one you never risked living.

~ *Growth: Poetry* ~

Sorting Through the Growth:
No Regrets

April 06, 2020

There have been moments of
sweet & deserved victory ..
& moments of bitter anger & pain ..
But ..
in every moment ..
there was God.
So ..
For every moment ..
I am thankful.
For every moment ..
God ..
I am grateful.
No Regrets.

"What are you desperate for?"

March 23, 2020

I am desperate for growth,
for love & peace ..
for a serenity so deep ..
nothing could throw off
my balance or sleep ..

I hunger to change the toxic behaviors
that dwell within me ..
to breakdown the walls I built ..
to protect & hide me ..

Desperate to heal ..
all those I meet ..
by being love ..
in every aspect they seek ..

Reminding strangers ..
& ones I hold close ..
"don't give up.. I promise ..
don't abandon hope"

It is in my soul's desperation ..
where I am anxious to save ..
every living being ..
from a love starvation ..

To give all that I have to give ..
to make someone's life feel worthy ..
when they carry nothing but doubt ..
to stop them from questioning ..
& show them what love is really
all about ..

No judgement, I promise ..
no conditions, I promise ..
no questions asked ..
I promise ..

Second chances ..
I promise.

To be ignorant & naïve is bliss

February 18, 2020

"Don't let the ugly in others, kill the beauty in you." - Aletheia Liola

I honestly couldn't tell you
if the girl in this picture
is in the slightest the
same woman
who writes this to you now.
Her dimples, & eyes may
twinkle the same,
& her smile still what
people remember her for.

10 years ago: 03/08/2010

But I can't deny that she wasn't
running from or towards something –
towards everything she always prayed for –
& away from all that reminded her
of how far her dreams really were ..
20 years old ..
In love with potential
y con todas las promesas que el diablo le dijo ..

Looking at this picture –
I'm reminded of the hope that lived inside me –
despite the fear of taking this risk.

{ 132 }

To be ignorant & naive is bliss ..
Thru hell & back .. she went ..
10 years pass, & yet ..
Her dimples & eyes still twinkle the same,
her smile still what people remember her for.

Illuminating the path I leave
w rose petals & seeds ..
& maybe one day,
they'll name a garden after me.

xo sabrina

It's beautiful when you can unlearn your own toxicity.
To radiate a healing love for yourself so genuine -
that when people see you, they see how your life reflects
how much **YOU MEAN TO YOU!**
My life is my greatest work - my portfolio.

xo sabrina

I make magic happen & like a gypsy ..
I follow my heart to faraway places ..
& as I journey through the lives of
so many beautiful souls ..
I scatter pieces of gold glitter & bold.

xo sabrina

Your intuition is speaking to you ..
Don't be afraid to step all the way out your bubble girl –
I promise you – nothing evil will come of it.
Only good can come from what your spirit is telling you.
Trust yourself.

xo sabrina

Transformation requires a lot of pressure
& a tower moment to force you into a new reality.
It's a battle, a test .. to try & force you into defeat.
Many people succumb to their victim mentalities
of lack & are unable to fight the heat,
melting & conforming to the ways of this world.
However, a select few, like steel,
are sharpened by the fire & reborn through it.

xo sabrina

you are a tree

September 02, 2020

There is no rush or right time to accomplish your goals.
Let go of society's perspective on where you should be
by a certain age.
Life is a forever evolving journey
towards our greatest self.
You will get there, on your time.
The trees are never intimidated when the grass
& flowers grow & bloom ..
The tree is strong, deep, & tall.
It carries years of age & can outlast many seasons ..
So trust chica ..
There may be flowers blooming faster all around you..
but you, *mi querida*..
are a tree..
strong, bold, & wise.
Your time is coming.
Don't rush, don't worry, just live
& enjoy the beauty in this moment.

My message will fall on deaf ears everyday – still ..
there will be one heart somewhere
who needs what I have to say .. so ..
I will continue to share my story, my passion
& walk in my soul's purpose ..
I will continue to journey this lonely road
for that one heart who will hear me.

xo sabrina

3D physical reset

November 12, 2022

Sometimes you're forced to shed who you used to be
through a 3D physical reset because who you're
becoming needs enough space to step through
in order for you to make these next moves ..

I am finding myself at a disconnect w
a lot of people I used to feel close to ..

I am realizing a shift has happened within myself
that desired certain things/goals/ideas etc.

I am navigating this sickness circulating my body w
a gentle gratitude .. because I know when this virus
is released from within me .. my old self will go w it ..

I am patient, but eager .. my soul hungers for growth ..
to further expand herself in wisdom through
the pains of my errors & the risks of my love ..

Like a marriage, I work through myself ..
in sickness & in health ..
like a player, I am loyal to thyself.

live with intention

January 03, 2023

Allow the love to grow, the peace to flow ..
& the innerstanding to unfold ..
Life is meant to be savored ..
Do not rush your pleasure,
your joy, your time ..
To be present is to be aware
& to be aware is to be patient w what's to come ..
Knowing you cannot rush anything meant to last -
Strength is built over time ..
Plant the seeds & enjoy the watering of each day ..
Time will pass - so live it -
intentionally.
Make each moment just as important as the last.

Vivir su vida mis amores, life is hella short ..
Do all the things, take all the risks ..
Don't hold back, don't wait for the perfect moment ..
El tiempo se va pasar - whether you want it to or not ..
Learn, explore, read, travel ..
Do it all, alone *o con sus amigos* ..
But whatever you do,
don't be the reason you never lived a life you love.

xo sabrina

Vulnerability is me wearing
my heart on my sleeve ..
no shame in my desires or past pain,
exposing my transgressions ..
through writing,
may the world decipher my disposition ..
just tryna instill hope
for those tryna figure out this game -
la vida ..
I don't play this shit in vain.

xo sabrina

~ Growth: Thought Pieces~

Healers are Human

September 21 & November 15, 2021

It's so important to choose a Healer who is genuine in their healing & journey, but also acknowledge that **NO ONE** is perfect - including us Healers! The healing **NEVER ENDS.** The struggles don't stop, but we are aware of our process & we now know & have the tools needed to work through the moments of discomfort. Realize that we are just like you - our paths may be different & our purpose may not look similar - but we are not exempt from the human experience & its raw reality of pain & down fall.

Choose your Healer wisely - but always choose w **GRACE** & compassion. They may still be sorting through some things, but it doesn't discredit their wisdom or their skills & divine calling to share their experiences & the tools that can help you heal as well.

People often look to me for inspiration & advice, but also have a tendency to think that my life is absolutely put together & that I've got it all figured out. But the truth is I'm still a mess, I'm still trying to heal from the traumas of my childhood, my first marriage, & even my own self-inflicted mistakes. I still have days that I cry wondering *"why"*, I still have days of feeling imposter syndrome & failing so many. I still get ghosted, played & lied to, I still attract hurt people full of selfish intentions who just want me for an ego boost. I am still too deep, too much, too loving, too soft, & too good to be true for many. I still don't have a perfect credit score, & I still feel the pressures of not being good enough every once in while.

BUT ..

I now have the level of awareness to stop & reflect & not allow these things to define my worth, to minimize my dopeness or distract me from the divine purpose God has entrusted me w. I am faithful to my vulnerability & share openly once God has done His work in me because I know that my life is a testimony that so many need. To realize that beauty is not exempt from flaws & imperfections.. is what makes us so beautiful. No one has the exact flaws or hot mess that we have. Wisdom is gained through the imperfections not perfection. We have to stop thinking that the ones handing out advice are 100% put together. No, we are human, we still have chaos - we've just learned to cruise through it w faith, knowing this is only another seed to be planted for growth & bloom. We have learned to transmute the chaos into wisdom & share it w you.

My character has been tested & my faith has been challenged.. My emotions have been vulnerable to attacks.. but all of the learning I've done over the years has really come through for me. Just really soaking into my heart & mind & finding peace despite the situations that have tested me, has really kept me grounded. Remaining calm & positive & coaching myself:

"Okay, take a deep breath .. Now what is this trying to teach me? How much control do I have over changing this? None? Then be still & know that all that is yours will remain so. & All that needs to leave – let it go."

Not overreacting & not allowing my emotions to dictate my attitude & actions has truly been my saving grace. I no longer fear or worry, I embrace all that comes my way – the good, the bad & all that's in between.

Just a reminder:

You are allowed to change your mind.
You're allowed to switch up your opinion,
your style, your position, all of it.
To grow & elevate is to **not** remain the same.
Don't mind the ones who are trippin about you acting different ..
The ones still holding onto what you said the other day,
the mistakes you made, or the actions you took
when you were less aware ..
Growth is known to be offensive to those
choosing to stay stagnant.

xo sabrina

Perception

Over the last year & a half I've come to the deep understanding of how powerful our own perceptions are & the way they can heavily influence our attitude in how we react to people & situations. & Even more powerfully how walking into certain situations with a preconceived idea of the outcome or vibe can actually attract THAT EXACT outcome. When you wake up in the morning – that "wrong side of the bed" is a perception & tone that we PLACE & set for the rest of the day. Becoming aware of the thoughts we process that limit ourselves & the way we CARRY those thoughts subconsciously throughout our daily experiences is the first step to reframing our mindset.

We have to practice seeing the positive in learning the lessons within our struggles & allow ourselves the freedom to let go of that which does not control, define, or value us. This can really help w creating a more positive day. Walk into the day w the mentality that all that happens is **NOT HAPPENING TO YOU BUT FOR YOU.**

How can this help w your own alignment?
How can today bring growth?

Today you *WILL* have a positive day no matter what happens – because you will make sure of it.

I have spent the last decade living a life of constant change & adventure, of both peace & chaos - exploring my impulsive ideas of taking a risk & never being afraid to take leaps of insurmountable faith.. but as I get older I desire more & more to be still, to slow down, & to enjoy the moment w people I love who love me back. With the ones who make life worth living. Yes, chasing dreams is always a *must* & now that I am fully grounded in pursuit of growth & living out my passions day by day - I just want to make sure I don't forget that none of this would mean anything w out all of the people I love. Life is meant to be lived - & setting healthy boundaries will always be necessary, but don't spend so much time choosing only for yourself that you stop choosing others. I left California for the second time in 2020 because God had lessons & experiences to show & teach me. It has been a beautiful two years in the Midwest of crazy spiritual ascension, physical, & mental transformation, & growth. & Now more than anything - all I can see is how much my family needs me & I need them no matter how independent & go getter that I am. I don't want to look back one day & regret the years I spent chasing my monetary dreams & adventures & realize I have no years left to share w my grandparents or people I care about. Maybe another adventure will be calling me somewhere else one day, who knows, but I know my next adventure is back home in California watching my nieces & nephews grow & spending whatever time I have left w my grandparents.

If you are able to speak your wisdom & testimony & connect dots on the lessons you learned, you are ready! Tomorrow may never come, share your story **now** because so much healing is wrapped in those experiences that will inspire those you don't even know. I used to doubt what I wanted to share because I felt like I needed to be MORE healed or MORE moved on from situations, but then I met someone who believed in me. They told me my gifts & I were needed, just as I was. Through this process of sharing my story I have found more healing. I've come to this place of accepting myself even though I'm still processing my traumas. Honestly, I still have so much more to learn. Allow me to be that person for you,

YOU ARE NEEDED JUST AS YOU ARE.

The Lesson:

**SHOW UP NO MATTER WHAT STAGE
YOU ARE IN YOUR HEALING.
THE WORLD NEEDS WHAT YOU'RE GIVING!**

Live like Kobe

It is in being our authentic selves .. that we inspire others to be as well. Amongst the most recent tragedy of losing Kobe Bryant, I have been reading on social media how much he inspired so many people. People have come out w their personal testimonies in how he helped them overcome fears they were otherwise afraid to face. Some even announced how Kobe was the hero & role model they didn't have at home growing up. Kobe embodied the perseverance & courage a lot of us needed as kids, because a lot of us didn't know what it meant to believe in our dreams.

KOBE IS A LEGACY.

If we all took that *"Mamba Mentality"* & applied it to our own work ethic & daily lives – we could all inspire even JUST ONE person, to do the same. Imagine the impact that ONE person made! Now imagine if we all could make small impacts everyday amongst our daily community w others. At our schools, jobs, our train commutes to work, our interaction with the barista at the coffee shop, etc..

Your place in the world is NEVER TOO SMALL to change a life. So go out there – & live like KOBE!

Allow things to unfold, let go of the need to manipulate or control situations w your fear, ego, &/or trauma constructed paradigms. Set the goals, do the work, & trust the timing of your journey! When we pair manifestation w faith, & disciplined aligned actions, beautiful things, opportunities, & people organically find their presence alongside you. You don't need to worry or stress, as long as you are walking within your own self-proclaimed truth & divine purpose - there is nothing you cannot do, overcome, create or build. Trust what your intuition is telling you, trust you know where you are going even if you are still tryna figure out how to get there. Your consciousness is aware of what's to come before you may understand it & that's what makes this life journey so beautiful. There will always be more to learn, more to uncover, more to decipher & decode, more to work towards, & more love to feel! So work through it, rest in it, enjoy the present, live as though your future is already here, **& KEEP GOING!**

Writing is one of my major expression gifts/tools within my purpose & path .. & sometimes I doubt sharing my thoughts/writing cause I know a lot of people aren't on the same wave as me .. But that's a healing journey I'm on of my recovering perfectionist, imposter syndrome, & knowing my worth. I am still working diligently on not holding myself back from fully embodying the message I'm here to share. I'm **MEANT** to be too deep, too analytical, too much for a lot of people - those are all in benefit to my calling. When I remind myself of all the people who have come to me thanking me for being **ME**: vulnerable, emotionally raw, & honest in my writing about the softer, lovey things, & healing .. I stop trippin on what the unaligned are thinking about my depth.

I'm here for the ones craving healing, deep soulful intimacy, & spiritual love.

It really is a forever thing though.. Some days I'm hella confident about what I'm writing & other days I'm like people not even guna understand me! So I tuck it in my notes app for later.. But the right people will.. The right people will read & hear everything we gotta share.. If not - the message wasn't meant for them in the first place. Blind eyes & deaf ears may not hear or see you - but the right ones guna feel you.

Take it as it resonates love.

My mind has been on growth mode.. soaking in so much game & value in a way that has expedited mindset shifts dramatically.. Ascending towards elevated levels of consciousness.. Like a Gemini - ya'll know us Aquarians do not like rules either.. we live mentally in the ethers. I have mos def been feeling & accepting the duality w/ in myself as of late & I am elated w how much this has mentally liberated me from giving any *fucks* of what others choose to think of me! It really is none of my biznesss & I love it! I'm excited for how this has opened me up to so many new ways of thinking & perceiving the world & the effects it has had on how I love myself & others. 2023 is mos def going to be a year full of **duality embracement** & LIVING that fully.. but I'm not even waiting.. I've already stepped into it now! Ending this last full moon & 2022 w my entire mind & heart on my sleeve.. Love & logic led by knowing & trusting myself & the intuition I used to question. As I said before, I am no longer in the box..

I AM OUTSIDE OF IT..

& I can't wait to share **MY PEACE.**

Discovering True Happiness & Wealth Beyond Societal Expectations

The world societal belief that life's ultimate goals are: career success, showing off fancy material gadgets, impressing the masses, and becoming "Insta' Famous" have always been conflicting in relation to the soul calling I carry within me. The last ten years of my life I have experienced an internal transformation – a metamorphosis. It is through this divine awakening and conscious awareness that I have begun to understand and uncover what it truly means to be wealthy, happy, and at peace.

When I was twenty years old, I ran off and got married to someone I had only met in person once. Young, spontaneous and a definite risk taker – I took this as my chance to get away from the toxic home environment in which I was raised. My spirit yearned for a deep connection that could heal me from the abandonment and neglect I suffered through as a child. Under this mindset of dependence, I was unaware of how the search for love outside of myself would only lead me through the doorway of a darker room filled with heartbreak and pain. It is through my toxic marriage that I began to experience the loss of myself. In turn, it is through my divorce and shortcomings that I have discovered the woman I am aligned to become. To find this level of understanding and peace within my failures, mistakes, and setbacks has freed me in ways I am only now scratching the surface of.

It is my belief that the learning and home environment play key roles in one's ability to fully bloom in the pursuit of their highest potential. In high school twelve years ago, I experienced the damage a negative home environment can have on one's learning. This affected my grades, my self-esteem, and my life-long goals. As an adult with a passion for healing myself and others, I have read many books, taken many webinars, seminars, and non-credit classes in order to expand my thinking and my knowledge. My home environment to-day has been an important factor in my ability to absorb and learn information which I then apply to my own life elevation process as well as in my teachings to others. Currently, I live alone and have created designated areas for studying, meditation, sleeping, and for enjoyment. I also practice positive thinking, affirmations, and other holistic practices to keep my space free of negative energy or as we say in my Latino culture, *"mal de ojo."*

Through the wisdom gained from my life experiences I have received a deeper sense of self and have created happiness. I have learned that life's true wealth lies within my peace of mind in acceptance of my past, the daily gratitude and beauty of my present, and the optimistic hope for my soul-fulfilling future. I may not be considered "successful" on paper according to my past, but I am blessed with the success in that – I have overcome some of my greatest traumas which has allowed me to help others overcome theirs.

That is my life's ultimate goal.

Do it Now! If there is anything I've learned in life .. It's you gotta do you **FOR YOU**. Not everyone is able to go w you on your journey towards purpose fulfilling God's glory in your life. Your friends aren't always going to be down for the adventures you're ready to jump blindly on. Your family is not always going to understand the plans you have in order to become who you are destined to be. & You yourself may not always feel adequate enough, ready, or even brave enough to take the leaps of faith, but do it anyways! You only get one life! If you mess up, it's the experience that you'll take w you forever. There is nothing more beautiful about life than the journey, the memories, & the experiences. I rather live knowing I did what I wanted & had to do & messed up than live wondering

WHAT IF I WOULD HAVE JUST DONE IT?!

Live fearlessly, tomorrow isn't promised.

A lot of the time we plant seeds
by being faithful to God's purpose in our lives ..
even in just using our talents & we don't even know it.
So don't stop sharing what it is God wants you to share.
You don't know whose life you may be changing.
You don't know what generational curses you are
inspiring to be broken in families outside of your own.

xo sabrina

After sorting through my own growth & healing.. I honestly believe that things meant for you come when you are ready for them. Everything else is a seasonal lesson.. an opportunity for growth & expansion towards self-awareness. Personally, I don't believe in wrong timing when one is divinely aligned with their purpose & one w self. Imagine if we accepted the myth of "wrong timing" .. We'd be dismissing all that's aligned & divinely meant for us by holding onto this narrative that we missed out on something living in our past. I feel like you can accept that at some point you weren't ready for something in the moment that it was presented to you, but it was still meant for *that moment* in time, because you - in some way learned about yourself & in turn that played a part in where you are now. Acknowledge what you weren't ready for, but let it go. & vice versa.. Accept what was never meant to stay longer than it did & let it go.

Taking Control of My Dating Life

Over the past year, I've been putting my dating skills to the test & learning to identify when someone isn't right for me. I no longer wait around to be chosen, or wonder if they like me. Instead, I ask *myself* these important questions:

Do I like them? Why or why not?
Am I feeling peace or uneasy?
Does this person align with my values and standards?
Are there any deal-breakers?
Are we compatible for the long term?
How do they handle stress and conflict?
Do they prioritize their health and well-being?

It's been a liberating experience to identify red flags & deal-breakers & not make excuses for them. I feel empowered, respecting my boundaries & protecting my peace while still being open to dating & finding love. This journey has taken years, but I'm finally here, & *la niña dentro de mi* is proud of our healing journey.

The thing about being an overthinker, is that you not only over-think, but you also reflect a lot too. Thinking is a passion for me, to connect to the deeper meaning of everything I come into contact with is something I crave to do. My brain & soul thrive on understanding the usually misunderstood lessons & blessings that sneak their way in disguised as rejections & failures.

There's always wisdom to gain.

xo sabrina

There's something really beautiful & mind-blowing
about standing in the midst of your own self-awareness.
Like, *"Wow, I really see that growth in me."*
or
"Yo, I'm feeling really triggered right now, let me take a step back real quick."
It's a powerful position to be standing in
when you can find yourself witnessing **YOU** in third person.

I feel like this is love.

xo sabrina

Rejection & Dating

Something I've learned & reflected on in this pandemic, is that love is patient, kind, & slow. Anything rushed usually doesn't last & building a foundational friendship is the key to true intimacy & lasting connection. I have also become vulnerably accepting to the fact that rejection is apart of dating & that it is in our reaction to rejection that we are able to reflect & grow towards understanding ourselves more deeply.

This past September marked my 7th year of being single. Yea, I had a few situationships, random friends with benefits & one night stands in that time, but nothing that I can outwardly say was an exclusive relationship. This isn't meant to blame those experiences as failures, but rather to shed light on the lessons, wisdoms, & the self-awareness I have gained despite those rejections & heartaches. It wasn't until earlier this year, when the shelter in place order went into effect, that I came to the realization of my own deeply rooted childhood traumas affecting my adult relationships & how I viewed myself. I have also more recently found, that my perception of what love should look like, is extremely flawed due to the perceptions & paradigms my traumas have created. So this is where I draw the line. I am analyzing & reflecting on what I think love should be & redefining what it actually IS. I want to set myself free from the bondage of my expectations & fantasies, so that I may love myself wholeheartedly & be receptive to whom is good to me instead of self-sabotaging intimately dope connections due to my anxious-fearful attachment style.

Most recently, I deleted my dating app profile. I accepted that—although this is the new way to meeting people & the way in which the dating world has evolved to.. it is not aligned with me & the person that I am. I am intricately deeper than most, & it can come off extremely overwhelming to someone only looking to casually hook up with the swipe of a pretty face just for the "YOLO" of it. I used to feel like I could possibly be too much & maybe I should turn it down a few notches, but this only left me feeling bored, unsatisfied, & misunderstood. When I began to filter out the low vibrational & superficially led men—I started to place intention on what it was I wanted out of dating & the kind of partner I desired. I began connecting with souls that were more & more aligned with what I wanted. Each experience slowly drawing me closer & closer to self while also defining more clearly, what it is I like & don't like when it comes to a romantic partner.

There is a fine line between setting intentions & having expectations—& without realizing it—I began to confuse the two. The closer I got with someone who seemed most aligned with my desired mate—the more expectation I began to place on what the relationship should become. I began to fantasize using the depth of our conversations & their understanding of my deepest thoughts—as a basis for how compatible & aligned I thought we were. I confused connection for chemistry instead of allowing the connection to build organically—I rushed it. This left no room for a friendship to grow—thus the connection dried out & I was once again back on some dating app swiping a million lefts. I felt disappointed & exhausted at the idea of having to find someone else who may or may not want more than just a pretty face with so much to say. So.. I deleted it. I have never liked the dating apps, but tried to embrace this new route that dating has taken. I know now that it is not for me—& that's okay.

This caused some self-reflection. As they say, each experience is a chance to grow towards greater self-awareness & understanding. I am highly vulnerable, transparent & communicative—but I can become attached & overly hopeful way too soon. I am able to spark intrigued curiosity of something more meaningful but at times I may not always allow space for the other person to connect to that meaning. This is due to the rushed & anxious attachment I have of someone who finally understands & accepts me as I am. This has led me to the understanding of how my traumas based in abandonment & infidelity both in childhood & my past marriage—have shaped the way that I relate to the idea of feeling understood & accepted by a possible romantic partner.

As I continue to explore myself & the patterns of my dating life—I am not only recognizing my own shadow—but also able to see how much growth I have done in the last 7 years. I am no longer reactive with my emotions when I feel triggered, hurt or misunderstood. Instead I am respectfully vocal about my feelings, thoughts, & questions while also providing space for the other person to navigate their own emotions & thoughts within the situation; so that we both feel safe to disclose what may not always be favorable to the other. I also have come to the acceptance—that we cannot force anyone to feel something that they do not. We cannot always expect a great connection to lead to more if the other is not ready or not emotionally in agreement with where we want the relationship to go. I used to want to talk about these things in hopes to change their mind, or convince them of my worth & how we could really make this work, but now, I realize there is nothing to discuss. If we want to be respected, we too have to respect that others have a right to feel how they feel without objection or interrogative questioning. We are only in control & responsible for our own feelings & emotions—anything & anyone outside of ourselves is out of our realm of control. I remember being the "loca" who would try to convince others of my worth—crying & acting hysterical in hopes that if they saw & felt my pain—they would reconsider &

stay. I haven't been friend zoned in a while, & most recently it finally happened. Instead of reacting with how I am used to reacting—I instead found myself being okay with it. I was obviously feeling rejected, feelings slightly hurt—but I knew in that moment that even though I had invested time into this situation—I had not wasted it. This was the first person in which I was able to practice some of the healthy new habits I have been working on—& while it did not lead to where I was hoping it would go, it did remind me of how far I have come as a woman who once felt hopeless & unloveable.

It is okay to feel sad when things don't work out—& it is also normal to be rejected at times. It is how we handle that rejection that matters most. Dating is hard, dating is scary, & it can honestly suck at times. But, if we begin to look at dating as learning experiences to become better partners, whether that is within ourselves—or even on how to choose better partners—we can always come out of each rejection or failed attempt as practice for the real deal.

We connect with so many dope people in our lives & everyone has something to teach us—whether it works out or not—don't miss the chance to grow deeper within yourself—so that when you do align w your person—you have the emotional intelligence & skills to create a healthy friendship foundation that blooms into the love you've always hoped for.

Sometimes I read my own writing or listen to my own podcast & I cry because I can't believe how much I have overcome. We sometimes forget how resilient we are.. & at times I feel like maybe I'm not doing enough.. but looking back humbles & motivates me – because – don't even take this as cocky – but I'm dope as fuck! I love how I have never given up. Even when I struggle, I keep going – knowing I will find a way.. & God is always right there.. blessing me & holding me – guiding me & checking me. One thing I know – is I can always depend on myself & w my proven track record – I trust that I will never allow myself to settle. I deserve all that I desire – the best & then some.

Forever blooming.

xo sabrina

I don't usually publicly talk about my desire of wanting a non-platonic love with another person, my expertise & wisdom is in the healing & self-love department. But through this journey of peeling back all the layers & filling myself up with love & self-acceptance, it is also so important to acknowledge our inner desires. As we become more self-aware there are moments where we recognize that stepping out of our comfort zone is the way to the next level, more self-awareness, more growth, more healing. We begin to understand that it is not only in learning how to love ourselves that we find peace & ascension, but also in learning how to accept love from others. Learning to be okay with someone being able & willing to love us even in the midst of our own imperfections & chaos.

As I fall more in love with myself, I begin to see more of my feminine energy *YIN* emerge & this deep passion to align with my masculine *YANG*.. bringing balance outside of ourselves in the same way we carry it within.

~ *Love: Poetry* ~

You w out me

December 01, 2019

To see you ..
to see me ..
in what we are w out one another ..
the workings of our hearts ..
the outside view ..
an admiration of your inner beauty –
that golden heart you carry ..
the one you share w even those
who don't always deserve it ..
your kindness -
giving & nurturing personality ..
it is when I see you ..
hear you ..
being who you are w out me –
that makes me love you.

xo sabrina
loving you from here

This realm is fleeting ..
Quantum leaping.

xo sabrina

telepathy

November 01, 2022

To be freely loved by you is the
universe's way of telling me
it heard me when I manifested a prayer
to be found by someone who loves the way I do ..
the passionate depth that I have always
craved exists between us here ..
when I am doubtful, you have
reminded me that it is all of me -
including my sensitivity
& softness that you choose ..
I can feel you even when no
words are spoken or proposed ..
This new sixth sense intuitively speaks
to me when you are not okay ..
So I pause throughout my day to close my eyes,
place both hands on my heart
& whisper *"I love you"*
& to you my energy flows ..
separated by life ..
& distance preventing us to be close ..
but still ..
just know wherever you go,
wherever you fall to your knees in defeat ..
close your eyes & think of me ..
because here ..
you will always have a home.

Left this dimension ..
Floating in space ..
Searching through the darkness ..
a billion stars ..
Hoping one of them is your familiar face.

xo sabrina

normalize givin' good men their roses ..
we focus so much on the type of men
we don't want & need ..
that we forget to mention all the good
that the right men are tryna do for us.

xo sabrina

I pray for someone who genuinely loves & appreciates me ..
accepts me for all that I was, am, will & won't be ..
someone who understands me when few words are spoken ..
& meets me on my muddiest days w the same admiration
they meet me w on my brighter ones.

xo sabrina

to coexist here w you ..
of all the realities we could be ..
it is in this one ..
that we both chose to meet.

xo sabrina

Sundays w my beloved

October 09, 2022

Let's cruise on this Sunday,
wrapping ourselves in the presence of our love,
forgetting just for a moment
what awaits us on Monday morning ..
just ride w me my beloved ..
kiss my golden ringed hand,
as I smile at you from the passenger seat ..
my smile creating dimples
& bashful lashed eyes ..
loving you feels .. euphoric ..
this bliss won't last long ..
being interrupted by the chaos
of our ambitious lives,
but in this moment, let us be here ..
we will figure tomorrow out when the sun rises
between the soft giggles & whispers of our kisses ..
as we lay on golden lit
egyptian cotton sheets ..
your fingers .. dancing along my skin ..
creating goosebumps ..
between my thighs.

I wana be soft

March 21, 2023

I wana be soft ..
loved so tenderly ..
I no longer fear taking my makeup off.
ya'll can I be real?
I wana be reminded that I am deeply loved,
even as I heal ..
I wana come home & be held by strong arms
as life's stresses melt away ..
because I know I have you here .. to stay.

I want peace to flood my nervous system ..
when I lay next to you at night ..
I wana drift off to sleep so deeply ..
because next to you I feel safe,
my anxiety no longer needs to fight ..
between my heart & brain ..
because when I wake up you'll be there,
breakfast sandwich in hand,
"Good morning baby, wana bite?"

I wana trust ..
because I forgot what that feels like ..
I wana be affirmed & planned for ..
I want someone who looks forward to my smell
& the taste of my lips ..

who falls in love w my laughter
& the little things I don't know I did ..
I want the romance, the family, & the kids ..
I want the flowers & holidays ..
your family becomes mine ..
I wana be kissed randomly & sent love letters ..
just to hear how I'm always on your mind ..
I'm tryna catch feelings & flights!
loved out loud by a man who is
both humble & proud ..
to know me & to love me in all & every way.

I want the cheesy, simpy, sensitive love
from a man unafraid to tell me
what he's thinking of ..
both lover & fighter ..
a man of logic & emotion ..
balanced from within ..
his mind disciplined, heart an ocean ..
of patience & gentle teachings ..
a man who loves passionately ..
my smile .. his daily goal ..
& my comfort? a winning poll!

I want the man willing to climb mountaintops
to find me, if the world started to end ..
a man who into my cup, it's love he pours ..
& on that he won't bend ..
loving me entirely, my Godsend ..
the one who looks at me & just knows,
"that's her, my baby, the woman I've been looking for."

Loving you isn't fading ..
I'm still here drawing hearts around your name ..
loving you hasn't changed ..
all this time has passed ..
& I still feel the same.

xo sabrina

meet me on the other side

October 11, 2022

I hope if I never get to touch you physically ..
if you leave this plane before my hands
are given the opportunity ..
to caress your beautifully designed face
& look up into your brown eyes
full of ammunition & focus ..
that you visit me in my dreams ..
that your spirit doesn't forget
to come kiss me goodbye
before you reincarnate into your next life ..
but still .. pinky promise ..
we'll meet up on the other side.

dejavú

October 11, 2022

How is it that you are no stranger to me,
that you're familiar w my soul?
How is it that we knew,
but only just now ..
are we beginning to know?
past life memories are coming back to me,
you say you have them too ..
but were you really there w me ..
or is this all apart of my dejavú?

delicacy

October 13, 2022

Tastin' me is a delicacy ..
initially captivated by the aesthetic of my beauty,
you took a dip w/in the grooves of my mind,
fallin' in love w everything you find ..
imaginin' the taste of my skin ..
as I confess to you all of my past sins.

vulnerable

October 14, 2022

You embraced the beauty within the flaws I tried to hide,
took my insecurities & caressed all my fears from the inside ..
I showed you parts of me i was afraid of
because I knew choosing each other meant honesty
was what our love needed to be made of ..
You said:

"Be real w me baby, tell me & show me everything,
I'm not trippin' about those miniscule details you worry of ..
I'ma love you regardless, this love I feel for you is for life,
I choose you, for me you're perfect - flawless."

Your lifestyle I wanted to learn to understand ..
Papi, I wanted to hear all your plans ..
I just had to know ..
you'd be around when i needed your hand.

We all have a story
& a reason for where we are in life ..
it is not our business to judge others –
if you can help someone
& you want to help them – do it.
It's a cruel world ..
all of us have dreams ..
& we all experience hardships..
never forget that.

xo sabrina

forever, a moment, or a szn?

October 15, 2022

Some love ain't meant to
be enjoyed together forever ..
be it for a moment or a szn ..
some love is meant to teach you
& always to grow you,
either way it end up ..
we gotta take the lessons
& just let ppl be who they show you.

Teach me your love language ..
like an eager student of linguistics,
I am willing to study the dialect of your heart
& the native tongue of your soul
if it means I can love you in
all the ways that feel like love for you ..
if it means understanding you in ways
you've always felt misunderstood.
Teach me & I will learn.

xo sabrina

what if..

October 15, 2022

& if together ..
our love coulda just lasted a lil' longer ..
who knows what beautiful things
our unashamed intimacy could have done ..
the generational curses we could've overcome ..
the battles we could've won ..
bonded ..
like the sky to the sun.

they'll still remember you

October 16, 2022

Centuries from now,
they'll still remember you.
your name will be spoken on the tongues of men
whose ancestors respected you.
they will tell of your keen eye to
every intentional detail you planted,
in awe of your pursuits ..
your words will continue to find their way
into the hearts of women whose
great grandmothers loved & desired you ..
reciting your poetry in bed
w their fingers ..
like taboo.

I will always be mine

October 16, 2022

You have inspired my mind ..
your love is like pandora's box,
I was.. unaware of the power it held,
the healing & self-awareness I would find ..
my limiting beliefs can no longer keep me confined ..
dissolving with every energetic exchange,
I am coming home to myself a second time ..
something only pure love can spark,
reminding me whether I am yours or not,
I will always still ..
be mine.

el sol y la luna

October 17, 2022

they called him the sun,
& she drew close to his warmth
unafraid of his burning flames..
she was soft & calm, her name was the moon,
shining her light upon every dark place..
& w her he wished his day could be consumed..
enamored by her gentle love..
creating a deep desire his heart yearned to pursue..
but they had higher callings to live out ..
things way bigger than me or you..
he retreated back into his kingdom skies
as she continued to reign amongst the stars..
& every day as they switched places
from east to west & west to east..
they longed for a day when they could
surrender to one another again..
making passionate love for hours
in celebration of the battles they won..
infiltrating the boundaries across dimensions,
creating infinite ripples & vibrations
of a pure & powerful love ..
a renowned sense of unending peace.
erotic ecstasy .. euphoric zen.

a kundalini love

October 20, 2022

Have you ever met someone who made
you love yourself more deeply?
someone who reminded you of your flame burning within?
someone not afraid to call you out in the name of love?
holding you accountable to your lack of boundaries they saw?
someone you can show up to in your true state,
& know with all certainty they will embrace you
& the love won't fade?

This type of love changes you,
you begin to love them & life through **self-loving** you..
your life becomes this infinitely expanding wildfire ..
love begins to exude from your skin ..
your energy transferring to everyday things ..
you no longer worry about the struggles
trying to prevent your wins ..
cause you've got love rooted & churning so deep within ..
& that daze bobby caldwell speaks of ..
is the daze you'll forever walk in ..
your life won't ever be the same,
you'll feel so free ..
you won't wana let this type of love go ..

But then reality hits ..
& sometimes ..
you just might have to.
maybe not forever ..
but for now you do ..
in this lifetime ..
this is part of what
they were meant to do ..
awaken you.

a love beyond the matrix

October 19, 2022

Like a cliché,
let's be bonnie & clyde,
baby don't just be my lovaa,
be my patna in crime ..
but instead of runnin' these streets,
let's breakdown the constraints of the human mind,
create a shift in places where ego can't shine ..
humbled we roll into places of our people ..
killin' any false narratives that
drown them into the abyss .. deeper ..
let's break out the matrix,
escapin' society's oppressive grin,
I'm tryna be a fugitive w you,
get us on that "most wanted" list ..
this guna be a war we win.

wrong timing

October 21, 2022

the verdict is in ..
love comes when you're busy focusin' on your wins..
neither of us were prepared for all the feelings
that caught us off guard & rushed the fuck in..
our timing was off but that didn't stop us ..
loving this together was just enough ..
others may not understand so we kept things hush hush ..
not out of secrecy but out of the idea that this love was insanity ..
too good to be true ..
you love tf outta me & I love the fuck outta you ..
obstacles began to stack up -
making things feel uncomfortable,
fighting thru it met us w some thoughts that maybe
this love really was impossible ..
separated physically but I know you stay feelin' me ..
talkin thru subliminals,
saying I love you telepathically ..
& until the timing finds us within alignment again ..
this love -
you -
are enough for me.

missing you thru music

October 23, 2022

when it's you I'm missing..
I turn on a tune & sing the lyrics in thought of you ..
you're found between the breaks of the dopest beats,
my heart receiving them *htz* on a love frequency ..
I talk to you through the poetry of my favorite songs
& extend my love through words I feel describe
this boundless love in which I am so fond ..
we are music & poetry ..
an intimacy & love that is nurtured through the
intentional exchange of our music shares ..
& sometimes when we're unable to be in presence ..
I'll drop a few lines for you to feel through my instagram stories ..
& I know you feel them too ..
I love sharing music w you.

enlighten me

October 27, 2022

there is something so sexy about a man
who can teach me a thing or two,
open up my mind in ways I never knew or planned to ..
expand the boundaries in which I have been confined,
elevate my consciousness to the levels of the divine ..
he is a teacher who has mastered the art of being a student,
it's a love language he speaks as he pours into me
the hidden wisdom tucked inside his mind ..
damn this man is SO FINE ..
intellectually intriguing me,
stimulating me mentally ..
I love a man who can enlighten me.

11:11

October 27, 2022

every 11:11 I wish on meeting you ..
I wonder what you look like,
& if you like oldies & blues like I do ..
I pray that your heart is as deep as mine,
with the capacity to love
& hold me on the days I pretend I'm fine ..
I ask God that you are patient
& slow to frustration ..
that you are a man of your word
& that I can trust you no matter the occasion ..
I write love letters to you on full moons,
hoping that when you look up, it somehow
reminds you of the lifetimes we've been through ..
& in this one, I can't wait to meet you ..
so whoever you are, whoever you're becoming ..
I hope this prayer reaches you ..
& I ask God that you're not that far ..
estoy aqui ..
esperándote ..
cerca del mar.

love co-signed in divinity

October 29, 2022

there's a strategy to this mess..
a blueprint to be paved
as we navigate the chaos outwardly & within..
I am the beauty to your beast,
a soft space to land in times of dis-*ease* ..
heart eyes for you & an open mind to this ..
your right hand through the trials you face ..
like Sade sang, ***"By Your Side"*** - I'll stay ..
let our love create its own pace ..
purpose & legacy we buildin' ..
separately to one day come
& piece together eventually ..
no matter how long it takes .. day by day ..
we'll iron out the kinks along the way ..
trusting one another even through the pauses & breaks -
moments of long silences, as sh*t falls into place ..
we see the vision .. a bigger picture ..
because we both know, what's understood need not be explained ..
our love a home .. wherever we are ..
near or apart .. like a grounding fixture.
baby, this is only the beginning,
a chapter together pending ..
our marathon soon to start to infinity ..
cause you plus me in every dimension -
our love co-signed in divinity.

A love that doesn't restrict me -
can I freely choose to be everything I desire?
While you love me .. watch & admire?
The beauty within my soul .. bloom ..
& you .. a privileged witness ..
to the greatest love story yet to transpire.

xo sabrina

to avoid & resist what you feel
is to prolong your healing
& journey to peace of mind.
take off your robe of steel, love..
it's okay to soften up
& feel what you're feeling.
sit down love, pause w me.. let's rest..
you can put your armor back on in the morning.

xo sabrina

a love that chooses you

October 30, 2022

love has a way of meeting us in places
we are not always prepared to be met ..
the masks of perfection fading with vulnerability,
risking rejection ..
it is on their acceptance we make a bet ..
but real love,
love that is unconditional to circumstances & appearances,
doesn't need you to play your cards right or show up unflawed ..
it does not ask you to change or decode messages like a game ..
it only asks you to be honest with an authenticity unaltered ..
even through the discomfort & pain ..
cause circumstances always change & beauty inevitably fades ..
your face youthful & smooth today ..
& then crows feet at the corner of your eyes
when you smile in a few decades ..
there will be days of happiness & then other times -
months of challenging mood swings ..
your lover won't always 100% of the
time be on your same frequency ..
embracing them in these szns with patience & peace is a necessity ..
love is the choice to love in recognition of all this ..
in knowing that things will always change ..
be with someone who's love will choose to love all of you ..
in every szn ..
just the same.

the love i pray about

November 02, 2022

I know the love I pray about exists ..
& although time continues to pass me by
w no lover of my own ..
I still hold an unwavering faith in knowing
that God has promised me a love so real & loyal ..
despite the heartaches & false starts in the past ..
my heart remains soft & enthusiastic ..
surface level & small talk won't do it ..
so patiently ..
I continue to wait ..
in solitude I sit.

mirror

November 03, 2022

My upper consciousness -
my outer state of awareness ..
was writing of all the ways in which I love you ..
but my subconscious was expressing
the reflection in which I have begun to love myself ..
tears fall not because I miss you, although I do ..
they fall because in this paradigm of love
we have created together ..
our separation, in which used to bring me pain -
has drawn us closer to ourselves
& has inspired a self-acceptance
I wish for the world to feel ..
to know.. to ascend to ..

I see you at different stages in your life
& my heart only continues to fall more deeply in love
w every person you used to be
& every person you are forming to become ..
I am more me because the more you - you become -
the more courage I have to let go
& allow my inner self & outer self to become one ..

You are a reflection of me & I am a reflection of you ..
although at different points in our journey ..
our souls speak a language only we know ..
thank you for following through w a promise
we made on another plane ..
you found me here on earth
& who I am has forever changed ..
since that moment nothing has been the same ..
quantum leaps of healing into dreams unexplained ..

I hope we are meant to meet in the flesh one day ..
again, wrote this w my entire heart,
I hope you read up to this part.

There's a restraint we all have on falling in love,
& being openly vulnerable in the presence
of someone that gets our heart skipping
& divine parts throbbing.
The boundaries we have are made of steel ..
thick titanium, impenetrable ..
even w the most genuine of expressions.
You see, we are constantly on guard ..
always creating a reason ..
to overprotect our heart.

xo sabrina

oozing & choosing

November 12, 2022

the truth is ..
I am deeply & sanely in love ..
& now I feel love deeply all around me ..
abundantly.
saturated in every breath & thought
that is born within me ..
love is **oozing** & **choosing** me ..
& I am receiving & reciprocating ..
I am sharing & spreading ..
because w love my cup overflows.

a love that is immortalized
by the divine union of two revolutionaries.
a legacy so powerful,
the world feels the potency of
our love for centuries to come.
the GOAT of all love stories ever told,
two GOATs that didn't fold.

xo sabrina

I been craving deep convo,
just wana take a big bite
of somebody's inner thoughts.

xo sabrina

love me wild

December 03, 2022

love me wild,
do not cage me or try to tame me ..
liberate me through unconditional love,
allow me to evolve & bloom
in the soil of your acceptance ..
leave your rules & uptight
restrictions at the door,
we don't do limitations over here ..
you have full autonomy of self
& who you are ..
as do I ..
let us find liberation within the
extension of our open arms,
I want to see you fly,
I want you to let me soar ..
be very much you,
as I be very much me ..
love me wild,
in a world that is trying
to control & restrain me.

I'll tell the world about thee

December 04, 2022

All day I can watch you speak in syllables & rhymes ..
listen to your thoughts & philosophical mind ..
but it is how the energetic frequency of your voice
& the mere presence of your existence
sends my heart racing,
my brain wanting,
my cuchi throbbing ..
into a yearning ..
only our tethered souls can spiritually satisfy,
fuck, I feel you ..
even w my eyes closed ..
even in my dreams ..
even when there are no words for us to speak ..
fuck, I love you,
you speak affirmations of love & beauty into me ..
& one day ..
I'll tell the world about thee.

I have been loving you
since before the awareness of your existence ..
been manifesting you for almost a decade,
I can't wait to meet you my future love.

xo sabrina

patience

December 12, 2022

a love connection - a bond ..
that transcends the physical ..
highly spiritual ..
energetic ..
mystical ..
a radical surrender to self
is a full surrender to you ..
my reflection - my love.
I am trusting my intuition,
divine timing & the process ..
the same day you plant the seed
is not the same day the flowers bloom.

I love an intelligent lover who teaches me things ..
a lover who engages w me ..
a lover who is present w my mind -
not just when my body is present to their eyes.

xo sabrina

szn of separation

December 12, 2022

I am learning true patience & trust ..
in this act of choosing
to love every part of you ..
when words are few & presence scarce ..
I take slow deep breaths to ground myself
& whisper this reminder:

*"Our physical separation is only temporary -
our souls have promised to unite for a much greater fight ..
right now is a szn of preparation ..
I love you deeply despite our separation."*

los cenotes

December 19, 2022

If it is depth you shy away from ..
then my soul is not yours to drink, love ..
for my waters are dark,
como los cenotes en México ..
you'll have to dive deep into the earth of my temple
to discover the treasures of my heart ..
there is beauty in the swim,
but from the surface you'll have to go far ..
do you believe in the tales of **El Dorado** - the city of gold?
if not, I cannot unrobe for you ..
I need a man who is bold -
in search of tales never proven & tales never told ..
you have to have faith in such beauties unseen
for my soul is gold to hold,
but you'll have to dive deep,
& uncover me with your eyes closed.

this is a vulnerable & loving safe space,
we aren't here to "play it cool"
show me all the feels,
love me in all the ways,
& provide me the safety to do the same

xo sabrina

a soul of yin & yang

April 17, 2020

you see external beauty,
but I am a soul ..
of yin & yang ..
longing for
a divine connection ..
& someone who understands ..
the depths in which
I dive daily ..
& is willing to swim w me ..
mentally ..
before ever touching me ..
physically.

I will live fully

May 18, 2020

It's only in the knowing
that your soul speaks to mine
in ways no one's ever has or ever could ..
that I will know ..
you my love ..
were always worth the wait ..
& so my darling here ..
I live fully & unapologetically ..
wild .. & 100% me ..
while for you ..
I wait.

loving you

April 30, 2023

I'll never stop falling in love w you ..
at a distance your evolution continues to encapsulate my heart ..
intriguing my mind with a growing curiosity ..
wondering if I will ever tire of watching you ..
studying you ..
observing you ..
& the answer remains the same, **never**.

I have found the one my heart adores ..
time & space are impossible restraints for this love -
quantum physics are the only explanation for this
telepathic infinite connection -
much too mind blowing for the average person ..
words will never be enough to enlighten them..
so poetry is what I use to release the tension -
one of these days,
I promise it's your name to the world -
I'll make sure to mention.

no ordinary man

January 16, 2022

I've accepted that the depths in which it takes to reach me
can drown even the best of swimmers ..
I've accepted that I am like a tsunami
w a current strong enough to swallow hearts whole ..
it is in my nature to be bold, open,
& unapologetic in my femininity.
to love so intensely it could be said
my affection awakens one to heal.
I am entirely vivid, divine, exquisite, & all that is beautiful -
& I've accepted that not just anyone can walk w such
a woman who has embraced both her darkness & light.
for my love is a calling - a divine purpose to be gifted.
my love is for a man who is selfless in his journey.
together we will impact the world w our love
so fearless, potent & deep -
a trigger to the rise of collective vibration.
unafraid to love one another w a vulnerability so raw -
a love that transcends carnal romances -
a soul testimony everyone can see.
& in that revelation I've accepted that not just
any ordinary man can be gifted w the purpose to love me.

waiting to love me

February 16, 2023

& the truth is ..
I am not always this well put together
& some days I feel less than sexy
but I'm learning to love & embrace myself
no matter what I look like
or how much weight I lose or gain ..
I am accepting myself in every szn
falling in love w my heart & spirit again & again ..
reminding myself that who I am in the 3D -
is worthy of being loved ..
for my soul goes deeper than
what any one's eyes can see ..
I am taking each moment to live in it ..
to dance w opportunities even
if I don't feel ready ..
to meet people w every flaw
& all the insecurities I carry ..
because life is way too short to be fooled
by the narratives that I need to lose 60lbs,
get a tummy tuck,
& be dressed a certain way
for someone to love me ..

I deserve to be loved ..
to be embraced fully in all my imperfections,
lonjas & sagging belly!
cause what I bring is pure ..
I am a sweetheart ready to hold you
in your most vulnerable moments ..
I am a friend willing to support all your dreams,
I am a lover praying to love you
in all the ways that make you feel safe ..
& it wasn't until
now that I know & truly believe ..
that there is a man out there waiting to love me ..
simply because, *I am me.*

Can I be honest?

July 28, 2021

Can I be honest? just for a moment ..
will you let me be real?
I promise – this will only be brief ..
can I just unrobe from beneath this cloak of steel?
will you – just for a minute –
allow me the space to express what it feels –
like to be soft but not free?
will you listen, to the tone of my voice
& the exhaustion in my breaths?
give me a sec – it's all I need ..
I am tired. so tired, you see?
from the constant rise of my heart beat
when the butterflies seem real ..
from the sparks that fly
but turn out to never be the real deal ..
the short lived talking stages, sharing a piece of me –
are causing fatigue ..

This plague of "wyd" texts but no true leads ..
the disappointment is heavy –
& w it, this steel robe i carry –
to protect me from the sharp edges & careless hands
that can never seem to carry -
the depths of my soul or the weight of my love –
always desired but never taken care of ..
fumbled, dropped, & mishandled –
all I yearn for is a masculine who will stand for –
me when I am weak, sick & tired.
a man who I can count on so I can submit,
be free – ya know, loved & truly admired?
do you hear me? do you get it?
this shit I speak is quantum levels too deep,
ya'll ain't ready for me.

I've been exploding w so much love & acceptance ..
new discoveries finding me ..
my hope no longer feeling long distance.
I can't fully explain it all yet ..
words escape my comprehension ..
thoughts too complex ..
to just simply mention ..
within any normal conversation.

xo sabrina

Red flags

January 29, 2023

I swallow quietly,
tryna force down
the lump in my throat
as I hold my breath
trying to resist my tears ..
even w a good heart
I can never seem to
attract the love part ..

I'm holding back the feelings
cause I know this ain't nobody's
fault but my own ..
always thinking maybe this time
it won't be another false start ..
overlooking the small signs
that whisper:

"This man ain't tryna play that part.
You deserve the world boo,
& he's made it clear,
it ain't you he's tryna give it to."

with you

March 04, 2023

it's in the sma - gestures,
I won't say the "little"
things cause I know how you are about that ..
but in everything you do, I notice ..
& to me they're huge.. I appreciate all of it ..
especially being present w you.
seeing your smile every time you open the door,
playing in your fro as your deep inside me ..
skin to skin when we kiss .. here I am ..
connecting thru oxytocin .. but still I hesitate ..
cause how big are these "little" things for you?
are you stimulated in multiple ways when
my body is in vicinity of you?
does my smile light up the moment when I
look up at you during our tv show marathons?
do you find peace in waking up next to me?
hearing me breathe as my body rests beside you?
am I on your mind?
are you hesitating too?
or is this all me?
another one of my karmic lessons to add
to God's plan for my growth?
a testimony of all the things I want in a man?
only to be temporary all over again?

whatever it is .. I'm flowing ..
however long it lasts ..
I enjoy sharing space
& experiencing all of this for the first time ..
christmas will always remind me of ice skating
& holding your hand ..
new year's at home sipping
& painting in your living room ..
when I think about all of it ..
you're an answered prayer ..
a manifestation I wrote down ..
& even if this doesn't last forever ..
just know ..
I am grateful for you.

mi masculino divino

June 17, 2021

I FELT IT.
That **release**.
The **melt**.. of all my control unto his lead.
The way he communicated..
direct & with an assertiveness —
Allowing me to trust & flow..
To **BE.**

.. Less of the masculine energy that I housed within
& outwardly.
No longer needing to beg, remind, or plead..
with how He should take initiative ..

"I got this Bebé, no' vamo' hacer asi."

The tingles ran through me,
every time he spoke
in our native tongue ..
it was like the ancestors were tryna get through to me:

"Mija, embrace his Masculine Energy
& let your Femininity fly free."

Soft, submissive, gentle, & warm.
I had no issue allowing this imbalance of
my Masculine energy to sit back –
while my Femininity, around him –
became the norm.

The submission was real,
because a **WOMAN** –
I was able to be.

To express, to teach, to feel, & to love,
He embraced all this **softness** &
Held it high above ..
With protection, logic, & respect ..

His energy provided a space where I could
Take off my mask & let my yearning soft spirit
seep through my flesh.
No more putting this man to the test.

"Masculino Divino,
que hermoso que nos encontremos ..
Guíame ..
y te demostraré un amor paciente,
fiel, y verdadero ..
te lo juro corazón.."

.. pero todo a su divino tiempo.

xo, tu feminina divina

I pray for a lover

March 05, 2023

I pray for a lover who is gentle in his anger,
a lover who moves in love when we disagree ..
I pray for a lover who shows me **AND**
tells me how much he cherishes my presence in his life ..
a lover who can lead & sustain his masculinity
through his own confidence.

a man who loves me unapologetically with his heart
because his mind has chosen to choose me daily -
& he knows being expressive in this choice is my love language ..
a man who trusts I am not here to ridicule him or his feelings.

I am here to listen, to hold space, to love him
& embrace all of his bruised pieces ..
I am here to nurture him & create peace in our home ..
we aren't perfect, but our own personal healing has
made our love perfect through being patient, honest,
vulnerable, & safe.

& w all of life's battles ..
I pray I find a man who can love me like this.

notice you

May 23, 2022

This version of me just randomly
began to notice you,
after all these years,
I now see how when you smile,
your dark eyes smile too ..
I now feel when you are sad & feeling blue ..
or realize you are just as goofy too ..
my admiration for all you do
has inspired me for years,
but it was merely just leading me to see
how much I'm soul attracted to you ..
all this time ..
who knew ..
I'd find myself crushing so hard on you.

Love Bombed

March 24, 2023

bombed.
by the words, the promises, the gestures.
but who could blame me when the actions was aligned?
cookin' for me & always givin' me the time -
to romance & slow dance ..
can you blame me for fallin' in a trance?
I was caught up in you -
I was sure this love was guna be true.

the sex was **way more than** aiight,
had my pussy drippin' pitch'as of juice ..
my mind & heart allowed my body to give in - no fight.
mentally stimulated, aroused by the deeper shit,
this nigga was educated.

my moves just flowed -
no longer calculated or premeditated -
by the group chat of my girls
on how to make him chase ..
I showed this nigga my true face,
not the cautious mask I wore for the fuckboys
who sweet talked & manipulated
w no intention beyond my pussy -
once inside - a nigga was situated ..

you had me moanin' love cries,
as you left marks all over my titties -
& y'all know - I ain't got not bitties!
oxytocin had me bondin' to the illusionary connection
I thought we was both feelin' ..
but see - these new niggas is different..
doin' more than just talk..
they out here manipulating angel numbers w actions -
evokin' feelings & thoughts ..

so it's time to tighten up ..
trust that intuition..
keep God on LOCK ..
cause I know I ain't the only one
out here getting love bombed.

I wish that for you

August 21, 2021

Physical attraction doesn't mean much
if the character is flawed
& the connection is unstable ..
yet - unfortunately,
it's all most people are chasing nowadays ..
I hope you find someone who's eager
to swim in deep murky waters w you -
cause you deserve a person who's
down to dive your depths ..
someone willing to embrace the parts of you
that may even be hidden from yourself ..
the less attractive pieces ..
tucked away in subconscious truth ..
someone who chooses to stay
& love you ..
when all that physical lust shit -
loses its appeal.

I wish that for you.
I manifest that for me.

xo sabrina

leading me to you

May 25, 2022

It is here where we collide
into the depths of vulnerable intimacy
& soul penetrating love ..
leaving behind the fallacies our darkest pains
painted upon the yearning canvases of our minds -
veiling our eyes from the living beauty
that was left for us to find ..
it was in the unmasking of ourselves that we were able to
lift the veil of such unfathomable lies
& finally be able to see one another ..
it has been a journey my love ..
I have traveled through time
& space to meet you here ..
I have lived many lives before this ..
all of which were leading me home to you.

Even after all the heartache, trauma, & rejection ..
the many failed talking stages ..
I'll never close myself off to the risk of loving
& the chance to be loved in return ..
I will not allow my past & fear of pain
ruin this beautiful life for me ..
we only got one,
& I'll be damned if I miss out on love because
people didn't love me the way I needed them to ..
I love me ..
& that's enough to keep my hope alive.

xo sabrina

~ *Love: Thought Pieces* ~

Conscious Love

March 28, 2023

A conscious love with another, first ignites within a conscious love for ourselves. We cannot become aware of the garden outside of us if our petals are closed. Bloom within your season & extend your loving scent to the world beyond you. To bloom is to transcend the matrix & its conditioning.. to be whole with all the pieces of you that you have reclaimed. Love is not just a feeling, but an entire embodiment - a **BEING** in which you are continuously **BECOMING** over & over again, as you **CHOOSE** to face yourself & embrace all that you see. Conscious love is an act, not in the sense of fallacies & manipulated illusions, but a *choice* in which we **act upon**. I can only love your wholeness free of envy & possession, when I, myself, accept that I too, am whole with or without you. Reframe your ego & release your attachment to control. Conscious love liberates not imprisons.

Practicing a boundless love with another, we must remember that we are all working towards a higher purpose & calling. Loving your partner through freedom & autonomy allows both of you to evolve as both individuals & partners. We are a partnership, but we are also two whole beings with connections to make & friends to build with. Release control & ownership & love within a state of peaceful ease & trust. Respect is key & boundaries are necessary, but knowing that our lover's needs cannot only be met by **SOLELY** us (their partner), releases pressure & strain for everyone. Let your lover be free & allow them to pursue their purpose & change the lives they came here to change.

A healthy, honest, & committed to growth, loving, & forever evolving relationship requires transparency & vulnerability.. masks can only be held up for so long before they become exhausting & begin to slip.. both partners are like mirrors to one another.. both will have to be willing to accept that this is a no hiding zone.. all things will be reflected out loud & it may be difficult to hear that we have a lot to work on from someone we want to impress & be the best for .. but that's why it's crucial to understand yourself & all that you are embodying - even the parts that are subjectively not as "attractive" or even considered toxic.. & equally so - pairing with someone who is slow to anger, judgement, & revenge.. someone who is compassionate, patient, & willing to support you through your healing & growth - but also someone who will hold you accountable & will not tolerate toxic &/or unhealthy relationship behavior - as this only enables one to continue such patterns without feeling the need to unlearn & relearn healthy ones. So in this realization, I've learned why I have been single for so long. God has been working through every fiber within me - guiding me through a healing journey that has been excruciating, but I know that in the past I wouldn't have been ready for the Man God has created to love me because I had so much I wasn't ready to face.. I am still forever a work in progress but acknowledging & knowing when to take a break & when to continue dating are so important. So... to more healthy love & less toxic glorification.

I value deep conversations so much ..
To be inspired by the knowledge, wisdom & perspectives of
another person who shares a passion for creative expression & provid-
ing a voice to others .. is seriously what my heart beats for .. The
people I can share my soul w on an underrated & yet highly intimate
level (platonic or not). I love & admire the comfort that radiates from
around the people who mirror this energy .. so deep .. so dope ..
May our depth bring us closer to people who will support & under-
stand us in all the ways we need them to.

xo sabrina

I had to let go of the toxic habit of fantasizing a lover's potential. I would imagine our whole lives together & in that clouded perception I would overlook the red flags or their straight forwardness: *"I don't want a relationship right now"*

Instead I took their "not wanting a relationship right now" as a challenge to change their mind w my love, my attentiveness, & as a supporter of their dreams.. Only to have my heart shattered when they stayed true to what they said: *"I don't want a relationship."*

I no longer fantasize the potential of anyone in relation to me.. I believe what people show & tell me now. The only potential & future I fantasize about is my own.

I have learned to be everything I am: loving, attentive, & supportive (within a healthy energetic capacity) - w out the strings attached to hoping maybe someone would finally pick me *because* of these things. I'm all these things simply because it is who I am.

When I began to appreciate the present moment for what it is - I learned how to choose myself & enjoy those experiencing the present w me. In this moment we are aligned & everything after this will either find alignment again or I'll find peace & wisdom in letting go.

Healing & deconditioning our minds of limiting beliefs & our learned/reactive toxic habits is a forever journey.. Embrace your willingness to learn w love rather than shaming yourself for having to unlearn & relearn in the first place. Being patient w **YOU** first is key.

We are our first experiment.Being patient, compassionate, loving, & forgiving towards ourselves is where it all starts.

Sometimes, It's No One's Loss

October 06 & 26, 2021

As I've sorted & worked through my healing & personal toxicity, I realized that someone **NOT** choosing me doesn't necessarily mean that **THEY** are the ones losing out. I realized that it's absolutely normal to just not be compatible or feel the connection as something you want to invest in - no matter how dope or attractive someone may initially seem or be. We aren't going to be appeasing to every single person we meet & this doesn't have to be a loss to either person involved. It just didn't work out. Nothing more to it. Some shit is not always **THAT DEEP**. As ironic as that sounds coming from me, but it's facts. Sometimes it's no one's loss - we just ain't **endgame** & that's cool too. Stop trying to feed yourself this narrative that everyone is losing out on you. Just flow w life knowing that the encounter did what it had to in that moment - y'all learned or you didn't & keep it moving.

I'm a firm believer that what is meant for you will always find its way to you. No matter what roadblocks, distractions, setbacks, failures, or "wrong timing." Faith is tested & it's learning to trust that you will not miss out on your blessings, your person, your soul tribe, &/or opportunities. Rejection is apart of life, it is needed to help us grow & shape our mindsets. I know that my singlehood is apart of my testimony & purpose. I know that it's bigger than me & sometimes I wonder how much more can I really learn - but I am constantly learning how to navigate these societal constructed paradigms of relationships, dating, & marriage. I am learning more about myself, my flaws, my dopeness, my desires & more about how to help others. I'm learning how to let go, how to create boundaries & how to accept rejection w/out questioning my worth. I have never let anyone hold me back from doing me & accomplishing my goals & living in my purpose. Single or in a relationship- I will always lookout for me. & Even though I know I'm amazing - I also now know that my amazing ain't for everybody & I'm learning to be okay w that.

I am **learning** to embody a constant state of "love" w out the anxious attachment to people, places, & things. I am **learning** to embrace my heart's true feelings w out being attached to outcomes.. Just the vulnerable art of true connection & the beauty of experience. I am **liberating** myself from the need to anxiously control love situations. I am **learning** to flow into my purpose & into divine alignment w those meant to be here w me. I am **unlearning** toxic attachment & expectations, so that I can learn how to love within a healthy dynamic .. between me & myself .. & me & others.

It's a journey.. & I'm in it for the long haul.

Being vulnerable about who you are, what you've done, & your
past - creates a space of intimacy & trust w the person you are
sharing yourself w. I want you to trust me with every flaw & every
mistake. I promise not to judge you. I promise that I will love you just
the same & I will be there next to you as you become your better self.
I want the non-physical intimacy to be so deep that when we finally
have sex - we are connected thru an explosion of soul connecting &
body shaking ecstasy.

xo sabrina

When I am filtering for most aligned romantic partners, I look for depth, soul, mission/purpose, loyalty, patience, & kindness. Superficial love ain't it for me. Society has created this division between men & women because of all the materialistic & 3D physical standards women & men are expecting from one another. **Love is no longer ON THE LIST.** There is definitely a lot of people who are starting to do the healing.. They are awakening to the value of soul connections & aligned missions.. But there are still a lot of people choosin' up based on superficial based lists. it's collectively harmful to the growth & healing of one another.. & I don't speak on anything I can't personally testify as a witness/first hand experience to. Love gotta be deeper than material success & wordly recognition.. ause that shit won't light your internal fire & keep your soul warm when shit hits the fan.

How can they love me into understanding & peace?
How can my purpose be met w them by my side?

Or

How can I love them into understanding & peace?
How can their mission be met w me by their side?

Those are the questions we need to be asking ourselves.

Navigating Healthy Relationships After Trauma

October 29, 2021

Dating in a healthy, balanced, safe, & peaceful union is actually really hard. The irony that safety can feel triggering can be difficult to understand until you're triggered by the calm & gentle assurance of a partner who genuinely means what they say & really will *"do"* just that.

You may be ready for something healthy - but it doesn't mean that PTSD isn't going to creep up now & again to tempt you into self-sabotage. You're so used to being love bombed & when things slow down you immediately connect this familiarity with someone losing interest. What you're experiencing can be withdrawals from love bombing. You're feening for the high of being constantly overly showered in a short amount of time & when the theatrics are over, you're used to things crashing & burning.

It's not easy dating healthy after years of trauma - but **it's possible**. Embrace yourself deeply in the moments you find yourself overthinking, doubting, retreating, questioning, & self-sabotaging. You've been thru a lot, your fears are valid. Communicate honestly with your partner & express what it is you're feeling. You don't need to go through this alone. A healthy relationship is two people working together without judgement. This may not be the one sided situations you've dealt w in the past. Allow your person the opportunity to stand with you in vulnerability & help you navigate through these triggering moments. This is how healthy relationships grow.

I hope that if you're alone today,
you remember all the ways that love has surrounded you every
other day - today is no different. Shower yourself w compassion
today & send love notes to all the people who love you & have chosen
you to be apart of their life. You are deserving & needed no matter
the date on the calendar. Write a love letter to yourself like you would
a lover & express all the things you love about you. You're beautiful
my loves & I am grateful for the connections we've made.

This is my *valentine* to you.

xo sabrina

Here's a life lesson that took me years to set a boundary on:

My heart still big, my love still major ..
but it's not so easily accessible.

I had to create these lines that would protect my kindness & love from people who only took from me. From people who picked up the water pitcher I poured into & drank it for themselves w out leaving me a drop.. I had to stop asking probing questions because people weren't showing up for me the same way.. I had to stop being **ALL IN** for a lot of people cause they weren't **ALL IN** for me. Sounds transactional, but that's not it.. it's reciprocal. We can share & give wholeheartedly but don't let it drain you..

Stop oversharing & overdoing for people who don't pour any water back into your pitcher.

You are not hard to love. Keep believing in love despite all the failed dates, talking stages, situationships, marriages that ended in divorce, engagements that fell through, whatever it is.. don't let those situations stop you from believing in love. Someone somewhere is waiting on the chance to find you & love you. I know this generation has made it hard to find hope amongst the sea of endless options, but don't harden your heart, stay open, stay soft, & always stay in the vibration of love.

xo sabrina

~ Erotic/Sensual: Poetry ~

let our bodies speak

October 26, 2022

Lay me on a bed of roses,
soft red petals as sheets ..
as you connect to me,
like the perfect puzzle piece ..
in me .. so deep ..
don't close your eyes,
look at me .. we don't need to speak ..
your eyes are telling me everything ..
your long slim fingers wrapped around
my throat like a sleeve ..
don't lose my gaze ..
your soul is speaking to me ..
our breathing is now in sync ..
I've waited for this moment ..
to be touched by your hands ..
& sensually f*cked by your piece ..
your soul already knows me ..
now let our bodies speak.

intimacy

October 18, 2022

bare ..
disrobed ..
vulnerably exposed ..
not thru the sight of thy skin,
but a verb -
the undressing of thy bare-bones ..
invitation only ..
& I let you cum all the way in ..
you caress the deep warmth of
my sweltry throbbing soul ..
making love to my intellect in
a language I didn't even know ..
I release myself to fully surrender ..
I am a receptor ..
receiving you deeply as your wisdom
& love spread me tender ..
you speak me to climax -
a paradigm shift,
awakening to the knowledge of
a world so erotically bliss ..
I am safe.
safe to embrace a sensually potent
& intellectually elated love as intimate as this.

wet velvet

October 29, 2022

Lock us in the bathroom ..
the crowd is waiting for us out there ..
you look down into my eyes,
you see my lashes framed around the almond shaped
windows introducing you to my soul ..
I'm wet.. throbbing.. looking up at you ..
the intensity of our love is pulsing ..
the energy between us ..
like poetry in the flesh.. tangible..
we want it right here ..
you grab my love handles my soft skin like butter
underneath your big hands ..
melting ..
I moan softly in relief ..
yearning for you as you pull me close ..
you lick your lips & take a deep breath
intaking the scent of my pheromones mixed
w the smell of a light jasmine oil & amber ..
you wana taste me ..
you fingers feel the wet warmth growing on the
velvety softness of my pants,
you can't wait to eat between my thighs ..
I'm here to feed you *papi* ..
let my pussy be your delight ..
tease me ..
I'ma tryna cum w you tonight.

if pleasure is a sin

February 15, 2023

the smell of masculinity
dresses his skin like a pheromone
calling to the yearning,
erotic, feminine within me
my pussy salivates in his presence ..
I want him ..
full, deep, thrusting ..
if pleasure is a sin ..
forgive me ..
cause I'ma let this nigga in.

I'm in the mood for love

January 26, 2023

I'm ..
always in the mood for some ..
lovin', fuckin', deep throat -
I mean - deep soul - touchin' ..
embrace me, caress me, lick me ..
thick pussy juicy ..
wet ..
she drippin' ..
wantin' you ..
to be sippin' ..
from this fountain of life that sits
warmly between my thighs ..
slip a finger or two inside ..
nipples perked up as I
moan your name between cries ..
I'm in the mood for love ..
the nasty kind.

sapiosexual

May 5, 2020

Moisten me down w words
that roll off ya tongue
& kiss me w the poetry
spoken from your juicy lips ..
I wana taste you ..
suck on ya thoughts ..
as we share deeper than
deep intellectual conversations
that teach me more than a quick
hit it & quit it,
"wyd, send me a pic"
type of lame ever can.

~ Handing Out Roses ~

When we stick together
& support one another ..
w out judgement ..
w out conditions or criteria ..
we are a little happier ..
& we all have a better chance
at reaching our full potential.
it takes a village.

xo sabrina

agradecida (adj): thankful

November 28, 2019

to live ..
to breathe ..
to see ..
to hear ..
to love ..
to know ..
to believe ..
to grow ..

to feel the hugs of those who surround me ..
to kiss the ones who have stood beside me ..
the ones who held my hands & allowed me to be ..
anything I wanted & still loved me ..
unconditionally ..
minus all the judgement ..

my tribe ..
my village ..
from my cup – gratitude spillage ..
it is for them – I am grateful ..
blessed tenfold ..
a hundred times ..
I am agradecida .. thankful.

My SOLmate

To my s0lmate, my yang:

you (& shrooms) held up the mirror that reignited
the fire to my creativity & hope for love in this world.

thank you for teaching me invaluable game,
believing in me, loving me through loving yourself,
& seeing all my subs to you through poetry lol

I love you ..
in this life, the last life, & in the next.

sin condiciones.

go be great, my love.

xo your s0l reflection – your yin.

RE: Thank you

August 16, 2020

Though our paths are headed in different directions ..
their brief crossing was divine.
thank you for being the answer to my prayers
when I needed it most ..
for the ear to vent to,
the support & encouragement I seeked ..
& the financial blessings when I depended on
God to bless me with a miracle.
you were that miracle.
glory be to God.
forever grateful ..
forever you are appreciated.
I will never forget your graciousness.
always, **con amor.**

xo sabrina

RIP Tio Lou

July 20, 2019

how selfish of me to think of how much I still need you,
how selfish of me to think of how much this hurts ME,
how selfish of me to wish you could be here forever ..
to believe you were invincible,
all your stories told me so, all your stories of the past told me –
my Tio was going to be here forever,
you would be here to hang TVs, shelves, & move furniture for me,
you would be here when I needed a laugh at your out
of this **WORLD** stories, that literally how could that even be true,
but witnesses agreed, you were **CRAZY** & they were true.

how selfish of me to think I had one more day,
one more week, one more message to get a reply ..
how selfish of me to wana hold onto life like
there would always be a tomorrow.

losing you has been the most difficult thing I have
had to deal with my entire adult life thus far ..
today tho, it's not about me .. it's about you.

Today we celebrate you Tio & how much you made ppl laugh,
how you were ALWAYS available when anyone needed you,
how you were the life of every party,
how you touched so many ppl with your dimples,
your laugh, & your open arms ..

today is about how you were
ALWAYS DOWN for the ride,
for watevaaa!!!
My tio was there!

Thank you,
thank you for always making life fun
when you were around ..
if I could count the stars & bring you back,
I would because I'm selfish
& I'm not ready for this type of stillness.

I love you tio ..
thank you for always being there when I needed you,
since the day I was born you took care of me,
looked out for me, & made me laugh.

I pray that you're at peace,
& that you know you are loved & missed.

xo sabrina
"ghooooosttttt"

Mama

September 12, 2020

To My Sweet & Soft, Cuddly Mama, my grandma

Your soft & feminine nature makes me feel safe & warm, your cooking can soothe any heartache, your "mores (amor)" can relax any anxious & stressed headache.. watching holiday movies w you in the middle of a hot summer day, or sitting w you at the dining table while you work on your jewelry & knitting crafts.. are all memories that make me feel at home. Your pancakes & platanos have always been everyone's favorite breakfast to wake up to as a kid.. your sniffles when you're trying not to cry during a sad movie, or your sneezes when you've had too much dessert ..

The only one who can calm our Papa bear down when we've made him angry or the one to hear us out when we don't know what to do.. always reminding us *"it's going to be okay mores"* .. your warmth is unmatched & i know that wherever you are.. I will always be home wish I could spend today w you & papa .. but this pandemic had other plans...

I love you mama & thank you for creating a place we can all run to when the world seems to be falling apart.

xo your pooh bear

Grandma Gwen

July 18, 2020

Since day one, you have been there, never missing a precious moment, recording every milestone with your camcorder, creating collages of pictures to remind us of all our special memories, & there in ways that I could never possibly thank you enough for.

When I was going through my toxic marriage & divorce, you helped me find a new home for mental peace, you prayed with me on the phone as I cried processing the shame, the pain, & my broken heart. You have never once made me feel that I couldn't get through that chapter in my life.

My cheerleader as I fought through college & my reminder that God will always have our backs.

Your love, your prayers, your scent of warm vanilla have always sustained me & guided me through the darkest of times & the brightest of moments.

Thank you will never be enough, but THANK YOU. I don't know where I would be w out you. You are the most selfless person, I have ever known.

I love you Grandma.

xo brina

"Mija, you can do it! " - My Papa

As a child, my *Papa* (abuelo/grandpa) would always encourage me to pursue my dreams, helping me with my math & science homework. He is a Mexican immigrant (now a U.S Citizen) from a small town called Salinas de Hidalgo in San Luis Potosí, Mexico. He instilled in me the values of consistency, perseverance, hard work, commitment & faith. He reminded my sister & I that we could be anything we wanted, but we had to be good at it & to love it. He emphasized the importance of providing for ourselves & pursuing a college education. "Dream big!" he would say, "it is never too late, don't give up."

All three of my grandparents are my biggest supporters. They may not always understand my path, but they have never given up on me. Through my journey of self-exploration & restoration, through my broken seasons & blooming harvests, they are there. They don't have college degrees or glamorous businesses, but they are hardworking people who came to the United States seeking a better life. Through tragedy & circumstance, they worked tirelessly day & night, & now they are able to enjoy a comfortable retirement. I want to thank them, give back to them, & make them proud. I would not be who I am today w out their love. I am not self-made. I am family-made, love-made, village-made, & grandparent-supported.

~ *Music* ~

Love is Boundless Playlist

I've created a playlist with some of the songs I listened to during my writing sessions. Each poem had a song that I played on repeat while I wrote. Music plays a vital part in my creative process, so it only felt right to create this playlist for ya'll! Sharing music is one of my favorite love languages!

1. **"Do 4 Love"** – Snoh Aalegra
2. **"4 in the Mornin"** – Nipsey Hussle
3. **"Stay Ready"** – Jhené Aiko
4. **"Back To Life"** – Soul II Soul
5. **"I Can Show You, Love"** – Larry June
6. **"I'll Be Seeing You"** – Billie Holiday
7. **"Inside My Love"** – Trina Broussard
8. **"So Delicious"** – Pockets
9. **"Coaster"** – Khalid
10. **"Just the Two of Us"** – Grover Washington Jr.
11. **"Best Thing"** – Janine
12. **"Distant Lover"** – Marvin Gaye
13. **"The Look of Love"** – Isaac Hayes
14. **"Romantic Lover"** – Eyedress
15. **"What You Won't Do for Love"** – Bobby Caldwell
16. **"Safe and Warm"** – Rose Royce
17. **"Eternal Light"** – Free Nationals
18. **"Almost Doesn't Count"** – Brandy

19. **"Use Somebody"** – Kings of Leon
20. **"Help Her Grow"** – Londrelle
21. **"My Lover's Prayer"** – Otis Redding
22. **"Beauty & The Madness"** – Rexx Life Raj, Fireboy DML & Wale
23. **"Nobody"** – Keith Sweat
24. **"Corazon Sin Cara"** – Prince Royce
25. **"By Your Side"** – Sade
26. **"Wrecking Ball"** – Miley Cyrus
27. **"Fall in Love with You"** – Montell Fish

You can find the link to this playlist in my bio on my website & social media accounts.

About the Author

Sabrina Pérez is an AfroLatina Certified Self-Love Coach, Mentor, Certified Reiki Practitioner, Poet, & Spiritually Conscious Writer. She focuses her work on subconscious healing & shadow work. Sabrina has studied psychology, somatic trauma therapy, nursing, psychedelic assisted therapy, human behavior, & consciousness to help her to understand how to support herself & others on their healing journeys.

Sabrina began writing poetry at the age of 12, & went on to publicly perform some of her work while she attended California State University, East Bay in 2008. A woman of unshakable faith in God, she expresses gratitude to the messy journey of life, as she states:

"It's bigger than me. This mess I've made.. it's bigger than me. & God is using it - using me.. & my writing is how I share it. For whoever needs it, for all who read it."

- xo sabrina

Booking & Contact Info

Mailing:

Sabrina Pérez
PO Box 292521
Sacramento, CA 95829

Email:

loveisboundlessbook@thesabrinaperez.net
contact@thesabrinaperezenterprises.com
**If you would like to book a coaching & healing session with me,
please email me to book.**

Websites:

www.thesabrinaperez.net
www.loveisboundlessbook.com
www.achicaonamission.com
www.selflovenbloom.com
www.thesabrinaperezenterprises.com

Podcasts:

All Streaming Platforms
   "a Chica on a Mission"
   "xo sabrina"

Social Media:

Instagram, TikTok, Youtube, Snapchat, Threads, Twitter, Pinterest, Facebook
@thesabrinaperez
@thesabrinaperezquotes
@achicaonamission
@selflovenbloom

Donations & Support:

CashApp: $thesabrinaperez
Venmo: @xothesabrinaperez